Danny deBruin

Technology
Across the Curriculum

Half-Year Edition
Word, Excel, and HTML

Technology Across the Curriculum: Half-Year Edition; Word, Excel, and HTML

This book is extracted from *Technology Across the Curriculum: Full Year Edition.* Parts of this book are also found in *Technology Across the Curriculum: Microsoft Excel.*

The companion Website to this book is found at **https://techacrossblog.wordpress.com**.

Adobe product screenshot(s) reprinted with permission from Adobe Systems Incorporated.

Microsoft product screenshot(s) used with permission from Microsoft.

All photos and illustrations ©2016, Danny A. deBruin

Front Cover Design: Stuart Richardson, Luna Design: **stuart@lunadesigninc.com**

Library of Congress Cataloging-in-Publication Data

Technology Across the Curriculum: Half-Year Edition; Word, Excel, and HTML by Danny A. deBruin.

    p. cm

    ISBN-13: 978-1535277358

    ISBN-10: 1535277351

    1. Computer Education. 2. Microsoft Word 3. Microsoft Excel 4. HTML

Table of Contents

Foreword 5

Introduction 7

Thank Yous 8

Dedication 9

Microsoft Word

1. Microsoft Word: File Management 11

2. Keyboarding 14

3. How Computers Work 17

4. Intro to MLA Formatting in MS Word 19

5. Plagiarism, Avoiding Plagiarism, Citing a Source,
   and Creating a Works Cited Page 25

6. Computer Vocab and IQ: Parsing Popular Comuter Jargon 30

7. The Business Letter and Mail Merge 32

8. The MLA Research Paper: Pregame Show 39

9. MLA Formatting: The Expository Research Paper 43

10. Expository Writing: Grammar, Transitions,
    Prepositions, and Some Writing Tips 46

11. Setting up Stylesheets in MS Word 51

12. Working in Columns, Setting Leader Lines, and Using Word Art 56

13. Working with Tables I: The Sixteen Panel Illustrated Story 60

14. Working with Tables II: Women Nobel Laureates
    and the Academic Table 63

Microsoft Excel

15. The Excel Workspace and the Mighty Format Cells Palette 67

16. Details on the Excel Workspace: A Reference Guide 71

17. Plotting Charts in Excel: The Seven Deadly Sins at the Movies 77

18. SmartArt Charts: Planning Your Million Dollar Dream Home 89

HTML

19. Urban Legends: A Simple Web Page 94

Index 102

Foreword

This is the half-year edition of *Technology Across the Curriculum*. This book is a condensed and edited-down version of *Technology Across the Curriculum: Full-Year Edition*. The Half-Year Edition contains parts and segments found in the Full-Year Edition.

The book's purpose is to introduce file management skills, basic computer skills, typing skills, as well as full class lessons that will help students master Microsoft Word, Microsoft Excel and HTML.

Introduction

THE PUSH FOR STEM or STEAM—Science, Technology, Engineering, Art, and Math—has flooded the education world over the past decade. As school subjects are presented in a more integrated fashion and computer technology is as common in the classroom as a blackboard and chalk, there may be no better forum to bring STEAM and integrated instruction than the computer classroom laboratory environment.

This book was written after ten years of classroom experience teaching academic concepts while demonstrating the necessary computer skills students need to succeed on the high school and college levels. Moreover, these skills will remain with students well after they have finished their academic careers. The exercises chosen for this book were selected to compliment academic courses (with an attempt to have some fun in other areas).

Technology Across the Curriculum is an integrated approach to learning computer skills as well as reinforcing academic subjects that range from science, math, art, history, English skills, economics, ethics, and political science. The idea behind this book is to broaden students' academic knowledge and skills while honing their computer aptitude.

Above all, many of the computer skills and academic subjects covered in this book will not only compliment other courses, but will stay with students long after they have graduated and entered adulthood. This book was written with the classroom in mind and an instructor, but it was also written with the independent learner in mind as well. The step-by-step instructions with screenshots and examples will help any learner complete all the tasks within this book.

The first section of this book utilizes exercises in Microsoft Word to teach basic file management skills, keyboarding, how to work within the Mac or Windows environment, fundamental technical computer information, English and grammar skills, and how to write and format a research paper. The Word section also focuses on building academic tables, formatting with graphics, and using Microsoft Word with other programs such as Excel and Internet browsers.

Along the way, students will be exposed to concepts in science, history, English and approaches to writing, as well as other academic concepts. Once these basic computer and academic skills have been mastered, concepts in ethics, math and assessing popular culture and movies will be introduced in the Microsoft Excel section.

The entire academic and "real life" exercises in this book are directly relatable and complimentary to other subjects taught in schools. The Word and Excel sections place a heavy emphasis on language and math skills respectively while utilizing visual learning capabilities.

The final section of this book covers HTML basic coding and how to work with HTML files. It is a simple exercise and exploration of Urban Legends that will also expose students to something they already know: anyone can publish anything on the World Wide Web. It will hopefully serve as a foundation for more complicated exercises in areas such as Computer Science and Computer Programming.

This integrated and multi-faceted approach to teaching computer skills while enhancing academic knowledge should fit in perfectly with any STEAM program. The information and skills contained in this book will not only compliment school and academic life, but hopefully will be of value years after students have graduated, which should be the aim of any textbook.

Thank Yous

Books like this one need a score of "thank yous."

I'd like to thank the scores of students I had over the years whose input, criticisms, and opinions have helped shape this book (even the moans, gasps, and groans).

I'd also like to thank Claire deBruin, Deirdre deBruin, Dr. Maryellen Minogue, Dr. Phyllis Dircks, Maria Flood, and Barbara Carroll for all of their input and support.

I'd be remiss if I didn't include the feedback and testing group created for this book, "The Wise Council of Humans:" Shaun Malone, Kyle Crowley, Charles Gould, Stuart Richardson, and Brendan O'Keefe.

Dedication

For Barbara Carroll; friend, mentor and colleague.

Section I: MS Word
File Management and Naming Conventions

1

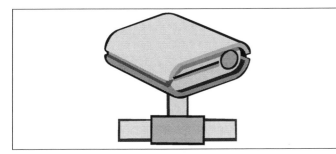

Figure 1.1: A network drive icon for Windows.

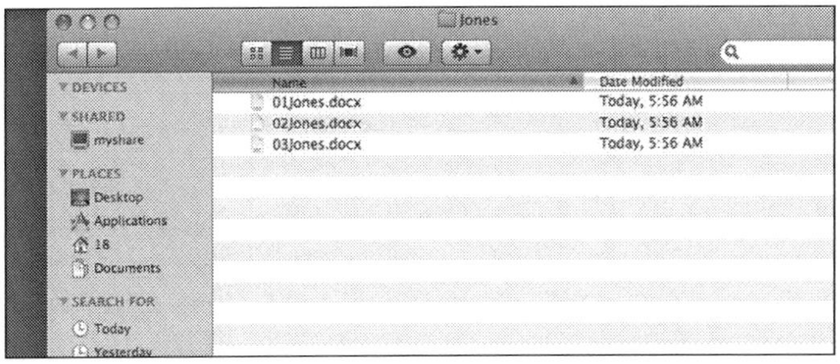

Figure 1.2: File naming convention in the list view for the Mac.

FILE MANAGEMENT IS JUST ANOTHER TERM for "staying organized." One of the differences between an experienced computer user and an inexperienced one is the former is organized whereas the latter is not. "File Management" is based on two ideas: (1) how a file is named and (2) where on a computer a file is saved. Users have to be aware of these two concepts both in the computer lab setting and at home or elsewhere.

There are a number of standard computer setups schools use for students, but essentially there are two working environments:

1. "Local," where students are saving files directly onto the "local" hard drive.

2. "Network Drive," where students are given a "user name" and "password" and they log onto a Local Area Network (LAN) and are encouraged to save files to this drive. This Network Drive is set up by an institution's computer administrator. This means that a computer user's work is saved to a "personal" network drive and can be accessed in the computer lab, the library, or from other computers located on the campus.

The benefits of working on a network drive as opposed to working "locally" are that files can be accessed from other computers on the campus and generally, network drives are frequently backed up, which adds another layer of protection should files become accidentally deleted or a computer breaks down.

Bad Habits

Most people launch a program like Microsoft Word and begin working right away. After they've accomplished some work, they save the file while not necessarily paying attention to where they save it and what they named the file. In many cases, students rely on program functions such as "Open Recent" or the "recent" list to open previous files.

In a classroom environment, if there is no consistent file naming convention or file organization, this can lead to lost files, especially if students are working off the "local" hard drive where other students may have access.

Also, when the "bell" rings, students may frantically save their files without considering what to name the file and where the file is being saved. On most PCs and Macs, the "Documents" folder is the default folder where files are saved. If a student is working off a Network Drive, then the "Documents" folder is the incorrect place to save files.

> *Note:* Most computer users call these folders they create (or that are prein-

stalled), "folders." Some computer science professionals call these folders, "directories."

Good Habits

Get into the habit of saving files first and then beginning your work. This way, files can be consistently named and more attention can be paid to "where" the file is being saved rather than trying to "beat the bell" and racing to the next class. Properly saving a file takes only a few moments as opposed to losing the file and wasting time trying to locate where that file was saved.

Creating a Class Folder (Directory)

Creating folders on the Mac and PC is one way for computer users to keep organized. On the Mac, a new folder can be created by going to the "File" menu and selecting "New folder." On the PC, a new folder is created by clicking on the New Folder command in a window or right-clicking and selecting "New>Folder" from the popup menu.

Students should use their last name when naming their class folder. If there are two students with the same last name, use the first letter of their first name after the last name.

Naming a File: "File Naming Conventions"

Consistency is critical to naming files. Having a consistent approach to naming files can also aid students searching local or network drives should a file "go missing:" it is easier to have an idea of how a file was named versus random or generic file naming conventions. A standard and sequential approach to naming files can be as follows:

Number + Student Name (01Jones)

And then the next project students work on, the file would be named, "02Jones," and then "03Jones," etc. By placing a number in front of the name, this ensures that the files will appear chronologically in the student's class folder in the "list" view option. In case there are two "Joneses" in the class, such as an Anthony and a Margaret Jones, the first letter of the first name should appear after the last name, like so: "01JonesA" and "01JonesM."

This file-naming convention will keep you organized and, should students have to either email or "drop" files in a common classroom drive, this will also help keep student files organized for the teacher as well. The naming convention will also help prevent students from over-riding other students' files in a common drive. Some assignments may call for a teacher collecting the original electronic files and having a random or disorganized file naming system can cause numerous problems for teachers and students.

For example, an assignment on *Tom Sawyer* might have a number of students naming the file, "Tom Sawyer." This not only poses an organizational problem for the teacher, but also may end up having files get "overridden" should two students name the file "Tom Sawyer." The first student uploads or "drops" the file in a common drive, the second student places his "Tom Sawyer" file in the same folder and accidentally clicks the "over-ride" selection from the dialogue or warning box. The first student's "Tom Sawyer" file is now missing.

The first rule of working: Stay organized!

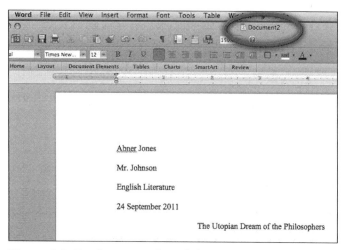

Figure 1.3: Don't start work and then save...

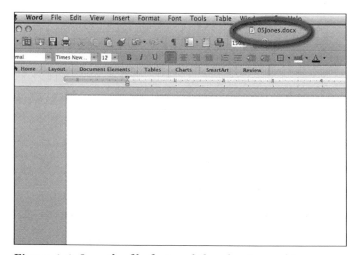

Figure 1.4: Save the file first and then begin working.

Recap

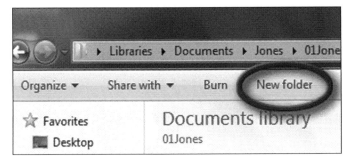

Figure 1.5: Creating a new folder or directory in Windows.

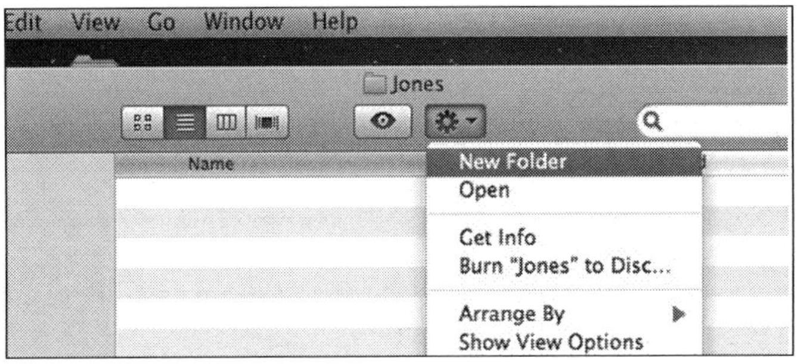

Figure 1.6: One way of creating a folder on a Mac.

Notes

_____

_____

_____

_____

_____

_____

_____

_____

_____

_____

_____

_____

_____

_____

_____

_____

_____

_____

_____

_____

_____

_____

_____

2 The Utterly Fascinating World of Keyboarding and QWERTY

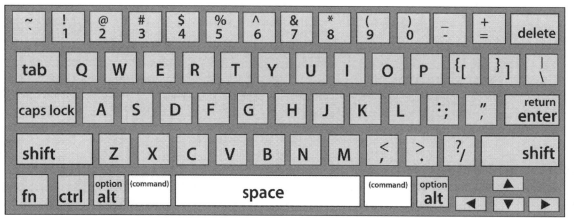

Figure 2.1: Did unknown forces plot to layout the keyboard in order to deliberately annoy young school children who just learned the ABC song?

DO YOU REMEMBER LOOKING at the keyboard for the first time and wondering why the letters were not arranged in alphabetical order? Perhaps you were in kindergarten or first grade, had recently mastered the alphabet and the "ABC Song," and then looked at the keyboard only to notice it was "wrong?"

The arrangement of the letters on the keyboard is leftover from old technology—the mechanical typewriter. This layout dates back to around the 1880s and is still with us to the present day. Most keyboards in use today are called "QWERTY," based on the first six letters of the top row on the keyboard. Some people pronounce it, "Qwerty Yuiop" (uuu-i-op), which is a way of including all of the letters on the top row.

The basic QWERTY keyboard layout has been around since the 1870s. First patented by Christopher Latham Sholes, a newspaper publisher and politician from Milwaukee, Wisconsin, and Carlos Glidden, who worked on the mechanical aspects of the typewriter in the same city, both men sold their invention to E. Remington and Sons, a firearms and typewriter manufacturing company. The company would evolve and eventually make electric shavers during the 20th Century.

The original layout of the QWERTY keyboard was proprietary, meaning that a private or non-governmental company owned the design and/or product with the intention to earn money, much in the same way Microsoft earns money for its operating system and program applications or Apple makes money selling computers and cell phones to consumers, educational institutions, and government agencies.

Presently, the QWERTY keyboard is "universal," meaning that it is a computer industry standard. The "perfection" of the QWERTY layout took about five years all together.

Slowing Down to Speed Up?

There's a controversy surrounding why the QWERTY keyboard was designed: was it designed to slow down or speed up typing? Believe it or not, some computer professionals debate this topic, as well as argue whether we should ditch the QWERTY keyboard layout for something else, perhaps a keyboard layout that is based on alphabetical order.

Regardless, computer experts know this: that the first typewriters were prone to jamming. The faster the typist, the more likely the metal arms on the typewriter keys would become heated and then tangle. Typists had to constantly stop typing in order to clear the jams.

Through trial-and-error and researching word usage, Sholes discovered that the QWERTY layout gave fast typists the least amount of key jams.

Secretaries were one of the first groups of non-computer science professionals to use computers on a daily basis. In the 1980s, as businesses began to migrate from electric typewriters to computers, it was more practical to keep the QWERTY keyboard layout than retrain secretaries.

Overall, the QWERTY layout is a leftover from a previous technology that is, more or less, obsolete—the mechanical typewriter, which existed before the electronic typewriter. It is similar to some leftover expressions still used today that reference old technology that remain in the American lexicon (vocabulary). Perhaps you've heard an older person say, "I need to tape a foot-ball game on TV," or while driving, "Roll up the windows," whereas most cars today have electronically powered windows. There's also, "Hang up the phone," which is a reference to the old phones that had a receiver and a base, when most people today use "wireless" phones or cell phones. And finally, most of us today believe in the heliocentric view, that the earth revolves around the sun, yet we still say "sunrise" and "sunset," implying that it is the sun that moves.

Now that we really haven't exactly settled the exact origins of the QWERTY keyboard layout, let's open a new document in Microsoft Word. Make sure you save the file correctly (02Your Last Name) and save it to the correct folder. Let's try a few short typing exercises. Do your best to avoid looking at the keyboard as you type. Mistakes are welcome.

Typing Exercise 2.1

In one minute, type one sentence, in perfect grammar with no abbreviations, using only the keys on the "Z" row.

Typing Exercise 2.2

If you cannot do the above exercise, type one sentence, in perfect grammar, with no abbreviations, using only the keys on the "Z row" and the "A row."

Some Rules about the Keyboard

1. The "Z-row;" where are the vowels? _____

2. The "A-row;" how many vowels are on the "A-Row?" _____

3. QWERTY and the Vowels; do vowels dominate this line? _____

The purpose of these nonsensical typing exercises is to give you an idea of where the keys are located without having to memorize the order. We know that the QWERTY row has most of the vowels except the letter "A." We know that the second row, which begins with the letter "A," has only that letter from the vowel family. And we know that there are "zero vowels" in the "z-row" (pardon the bad pun; saying "Z-row" sounds a little like "zero").

By now, you've probably thought about the keyboard more than you ever wanted to but, should you ever find yourself in a discussion about technology, the industrial revolution, and post-Civil War America, the QWERTY layout is a sure addition to those discussions that may take place in an American history class.

In the same document, try typing the following sentences without looking at the keyboard. Once again, mistakes are welcome.

```
You are walking down the street.

The last thing we want is a rotten potato.

I like to think we are finished typing nonsense.

There is always room for a little more nonsense.
```

The Home Keys

The "F" and "J" keys each have a nib or bump on their face, indicating that they are the "home keys." The left index finger is supposed to be positioned around the "F" key and the right index finger is supposed to be positioned around the "F" key.

The thumbs are to be used for the space bar and the "command" keys (on the Mac, a "Command" key is sometimes represented by the company's Apple logo, on the PC, the "Command" key is sometimes represented by the Microsoft corporation's "Windows" logo).

The figure below gives a general representation what fingers should be used to strike the appropriate keys.

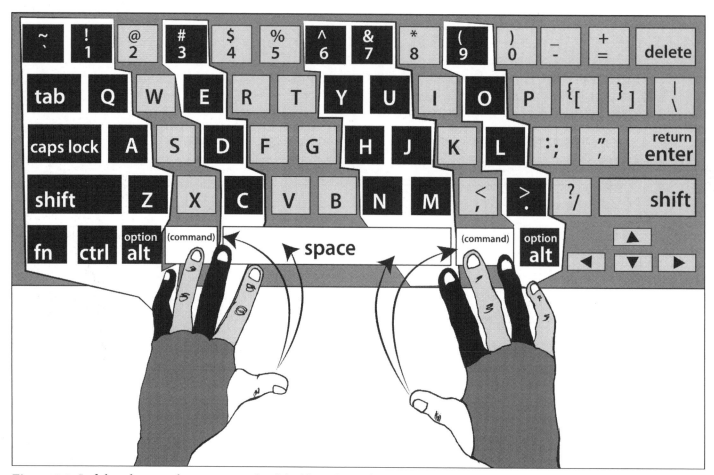

Figure 2.2: Left hand: try to keep your pinky (black) striking the black keys; your ring-finger striking the gray keys, your middle finger striking the black keys, and your pointer finger striking the gray keys. Thumbs should be used for "command keys" and the space bar. On the right hand, the same follows: try to keep your pointer finger on the black keys, the middle finger (gray) on the gray keys, your ring finger (black) on the black keys, and your pinky for the gray areas. It's not neceessary to get these "exact," but having hands positioned correctly will improve your typing skills.

Notes

3

How Computers Work:
The Keyboard, Inputting
and Outputting

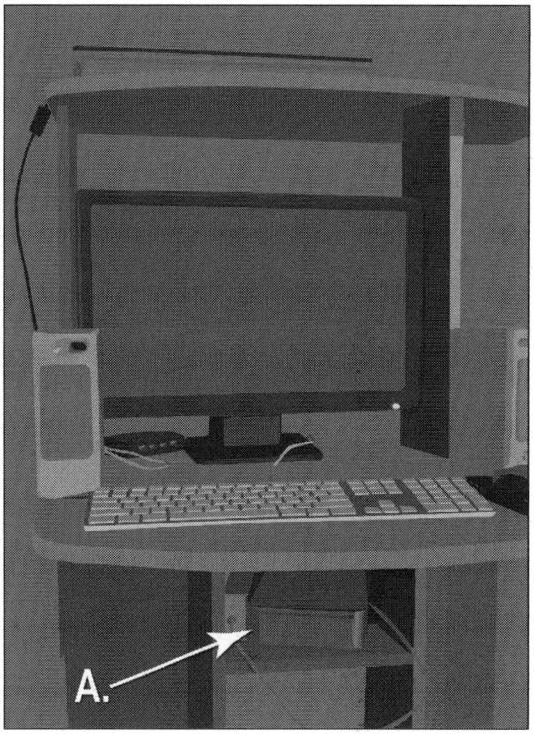

Figure 3.1: A Mac Mini (A.) with speakers, monitor, mouse, keyboard and a multi-USB port. The keyboard sends electronic signals to the processor, which uses binary language that is then converted to readable language via the Operating System. In the early days of the personal computer, some typists were faster than the computer and sometimes it would take a moment for the letters to appear on the screen. With the speed of computers today being much faster than computers in the 1980s, this "delay" rarely happens.

WHEN A COMPUTER USER PRESSES A KEY, a letter instantly appears on the screen. Behind this "action" is a complicated process that takes a few moments to explain, much longer than it takes for the letter "B" to appear on a computer screen. That letter "B" is like the cliche, "the tip of the iceberg," where there is more beneath the surface than what appears on a computer screen.

In fact, you'll realize your computer or "smart phone" is working a lot harder than you may know for every character that you type, or every image you view, or song you play. But let's discuss the basic function of the keyboard with the assumption that every other "input action" you make on a computer, smart phone, or "tablet," a similar process takes place, whether it is taking a photo, playing a video game, or listening to music.

Most computer keyboards have an electrical current running through them; beneath every key on the keyboard is an electrical receptor that is "activated" whenever a computer user presses down on a key; this is known as "inputting." The inputting "action" (the key being pushed down and then "released"), sends an electronic signal to a microprocessor in the keyboard that reaches a matrix, a type of "graph" or "chart" that is rectangular and has a bunch of numbers and symbols arranged in columns and rows that identify a number, letter, or other character.

Once the computer user presses the key, the "electronic shock" has been put into action. Next, that "shock" has to be processed by the keyboard's processor, and then that signal then goes to the computer's Central Processing Unit (CPU) where the "electric shock" is converted to "binary language," the language of computers. Binary language is always made up of two numbers (like the "bi" in "bicycle"), which are "zeros" (0) and "ones" (1). The zeros and ones are also called "digits," hence "digital."

Binary language works in a similar way a popular numbers-for-letters "secret code" used by some younger children works: where numbers represent a letter in the alphabet. In the case of the numbers-for-letters "secret code," it looks like this:

> 1 = A
> 2 = B
> 3 = C

And so on. Using this code, the word "cab" looks like this: 3-1-2. The electric shocks created by the keyboard, after being "translated" by the keyboard's microprocessor, are sent (input) into the computer's Central Processing Unit, which crunches these electric shocks into binary language. The first three letters of the alphabet in binary language are as follows:

> 01100001 = A
> 01100010 = B
> 01100011 = C

And so on. In binary language, the word "cab" would look like this: 01100011-01100001-01100010. Most people could not read this or be bothered reading it. So, after the word "cab" has been input by three keystrokes and the electric signals are translated to this binary code, it has to be re-translated so the computer user can see or understand what he or she just typed into the computer screen. When a computer displays or produces work that was "input," this action is called "outputting."

This is where the Operating System kicks in: a computer's Operating System (OS) takes those binary numbers and translates them so they can be read as "cab."

Computer Applications or "programs," or "apps," help the computer user organize and work within the Operating System. The entire operation is similar to a two story house with a basement/foundation:

1. The CPU is the foundation or basement.

2. The Operating System is the first floor that "sits" on top of the basement.

3. Programs or Applications or "apps" are the second floor, which sit on top of the first floor, which sits on top of the basement.

> *Note:* Nothing will happen in that house unless people walk into the front door (input). Walking out of the front door is also an "action" (output).

The reality is, everything you see on a computer screen is really just a bunch of converted zeros and ones represented by type characters on the screen. When it comes to computer graphics, a similar concept exists: a photo of the president or celebrity or a headline on a news web site is really just a pile of zeros and ones that were caused by a series of electrical shocks.

As well, your favorite song played on an MP3 player such as an iPod or on your "smart phone" is really just a pile of zeros and ones being translated by the computer that was (1) input and then (2) output.

A similar example to how letters and graphics are "made" on a computer can be found on the Internet and how Web pages work. Behind every web page is a code or "language" that exists to make the Web page "work." Launch your browser (Windows, "Explorer") and go to the View menu. Look for "Source" and another "window" will appear, loaded with what what is called "HTML source code." The concept is similar: a complicated code "lives" behind what appears to be some text and images.

On the Mac and in Safari, getting to the source code for a Web page used to be a lot simpler but for some strange reason, the brain-trust at Apple decided to make it more complicated. You need to launch Safari and then go into Preferences under the Safari menu. Click on the Advanced tab in the dialog box and then click on "Show Develop menu in the menu bar" located at the bottom of the dialog box (see **Figure 3.2**). Once the Develop menu appears in the Menu bar, select "Show Page Source."

The touchscreen on a "smart phone" works very similar to the way a computer keyboard works. The key difference between a touchscreen on a smart phone and a keyboard is that the touchscreen is using the electric current in your body to make things work.

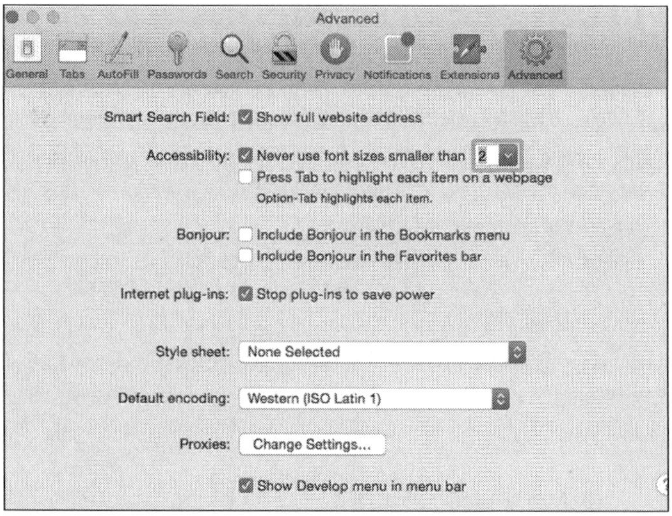

Figure 3.2: Ensuring that the Develop menu appears in Safari on the Mac.

4 Intro to MLA Formatting in MS Word: Another Typing Exercise, Too

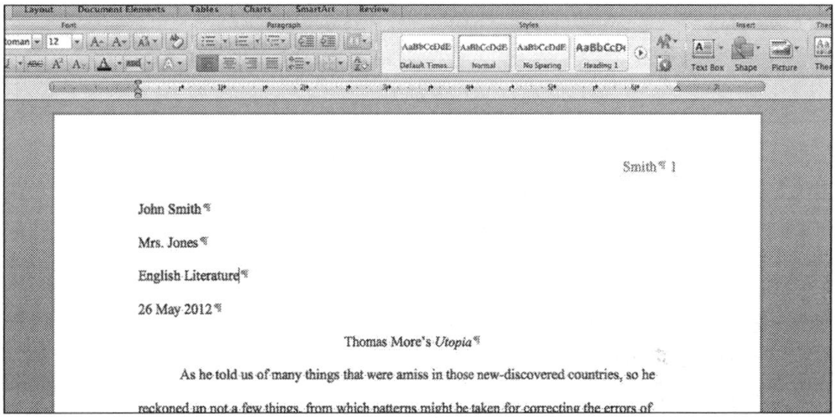

Figure 4.1: The opening page of an MLA-formatted paper in Microsoft Word. The running-head on the upper-right corner has the student's last name and page number, followed by the "**badge**" (student name, teacher name, course name and date), followed by the paper title and then the opening paragraph. It is double-spaced. Most of the formatting takes place in the "Paragraph Formatting" palette.

LAUNCH MICROSOFT WORD and save the file "04YourLastName.docx" (or whatever is the appropriate number in the naming convention sequence). Be sure to save the file in your class folder.

In this exercise, we will be typing an excerpt from Thomas More's book, *Utopia*, and then formatting the text in the MLA (Modern Language Association's) format. The MLA Format is a standard used by many colleges and high schools for formatting and citing a research paper. "MLA" stands for the Modern Language Association (Web site: http://www.mla.org/). The MLA is a group of educators that sets standards for writing and formatting papers in the humanities (i.e., English class).

Please keep in mind that MLA Formatting periodically undergoes changes and updates, so it is recommended that whenever writing a formal paper, "check in" with the MLA Website to ensure the formatting you are using is up-to-date.

Although there are other formats for other areas of academics such as history, the Chicago Style, or philosophy, learning the MLA style will expose you to formatting and writing standards necessary for high school and college.

***

Thomas More (1478—1535), often called the "last medieval man and the first renaissance man," was a lawyer, philosopher, and a Christian humanist who lived during the English "Reformation." When King Henry VIII broke away from the Catholic Church and formed the Church of England, Thomas More was the Lord Chancellor of England, the first layman to hold this governmental position in England. Prior to Thomas More, the men who held the position of Lord Chancellor were Catholic clergy (Bishops, etc.).

Associated with the Northern Christian Humanist Movement of the Renaissance because of his popular writings, Thomas More is a beloved figure by Protestants, Catholics, and non-Christians. More came into conflict with King Henry VIII because the king wanted an annulment from his wife, Catherine of Aragon. The king argued that because Catherine did not provide him with a male heir to the throne, and that she was originally his deceased brother's wife, he qualified for an annulment. The Pope declined Henry VIII's request, so Henry confiscated Catholic Churches and property and made himself head of the church in England. King Henry VIII desperately wanted Thomas More's support, but when More remained silent, he was arrested and imprisoned for treason.

Because of Thomas More's popularity and status in England, King Henry VIII viewed Thomas More's support of the annulment and the newly formed Church of England as critical. When Thomas More wished to remain silent, King Henry VIII insisted this was treason and had Thomas More beheaded in a public execution in 1535. King Henry VIII would also eventually behead two of his six wives and many others who opposed him.

More's book, *Utopia*, has been in print and read by generations since 1516. Originally written in Latin, it was not until after More's execution when *Utopia* was published in English. The word "utopia" roughly translates from Greek to mean, "No Place." It is More's book that popularized the word to mean "a perfect place" or "perfect society," a theme that is found in modern literature, such as *The Giver* (perhaps more "dystopian" than "utopian"). The book *Utopia* is a satire that portrays an "ideal society." In the new Microsoft Word document you just created, please input the four paragraphs. Once again, minor typing mistakes are not of concern.

Excerpt from Thomas More's *Utopia:*

As he told us of many things that were amiss in those new-discovered countries, so he reckoned up not a few things, from which patterns might be taken for correcting the errors of these nations among whom we live; of which an account may be given, as I have already promised, at some other time; for, at present, I intend only to relate those particulars that he told us, of the manners and laws of the Utopians: but I will begin with the occasion that led us to speak of that commonwealth.

After Raphael had discoursed with great judgment on the many errors that were both among us and these nations, had treated of the wise institutions both here and there, and had spoken as distinctly of the customs and government of every nation through which he had past, as if he had spent his whole life in it, Peter, being struck with admiration, said, "I wonder, Raphael, how it comes that you enter into no king's service, for I am sure there are none to whom you would not be very acceptable; for your learning and knowledge, both of men and things, is such, that you would not only entertain them very pleasantly, but be of great use to them, by the examples you could set before them, and the advices you could give them; and by this means you would both serve your own interest, and be of great use to all your friends."

"As for my friends," answered he, "I need not be much concerned, having already done for them all that was incumbent on me; for when I was not only in good health, but fresh and young, I distributed that among my kindred and friends which other people do not part with till they are old and sick: when they then unwillingly give that which they can enjoy no longer themselves. I think my friends ought to rest contented with this, and not to expect that for their sakes I should enslave myself to any king whatsoever."

"Happier?" answered Raphael, "is that to be compassed in a way so abhorrent to my genius? Now I live as I will, to which I believe, few courtiers can pretend; and there are so many that court the favor of great men, that there will be no great loss if they are not troubled either with me or with others of my temper."

Do your best to replicate what you see above and do not concern yourself with matching the four paragraphs line-by-line. This text will eventually be formatted in the MLA format. Some things to consider first:

- The MLA format requires 12-point, Times New Roman font. The margins should be one inch on all sides. The paper should be double-spaced and include a "running head."

- The first page of a formal paper in the MLA format has the student's name, the teacher's name, the course name, and the date each on a separate line. This will be called the paper's "Badge," which gives the reader (teacher/professor) all the identification information. The date's month is always spelled out (i.e., 24 October 2012). The first page also includes the title, which is never underlined, italicized, or bolded and always centered. (See **Figure 4.1** on the previous page).

- The last page of a formal paper in the MLA format is the Works Cited page. This page consists of all "sources" used for the paper, including books, Web sites, magazines, newspapers, class lectures, TV shows, movies, and any other "media" that contains information that is relevant to the paper.

- Each page in a formal paper is "paginated," meaning it is organized and numbered sequentially. On the upper right corner of each page, the student's last name and then the page number will appear. Should there be two students with the same last name in class, then the student's first name initial is placed after the last name and a comma following the last name (i.e., Smith, B.).

1. Input the "Badge" (your name, teacher's name, course name, and date).

2. Input the title (in this case, Thomas More's *Utopia*)

3. Select All (Edit>>Select all or "Command + A" (Mac); Windows, "Control + A"). Change the font if necessary.

Preferences and Options

This project will be done with "Invisible Characters" viewable in the Microsoft Word document. Having "invisible characters" turned on may be annoying for some computer users, but it is a valuable editing tool and allows users to see "non-printing characters" such as spaces between words, paragraph end markers, and so on.

Just as letters appear when a computer user presses an alphabetical key, nonprinting characters appear when a computer user presses the space bar, tab key, and the paragraph return (the "Enter" or "Return" key).

To turn on invisible characters for the Mac, go to the "Word" menu and select "Preferences." A dialogue box will appear featuring a number of options, such as "General," "View," "Edit," etc. Choose the "View" section and another dialogue box will appear. Make sure in the "Nonprinting characters" section, the "All" box is checked off (**Figures 4.2, 4.3, and 4.4**).

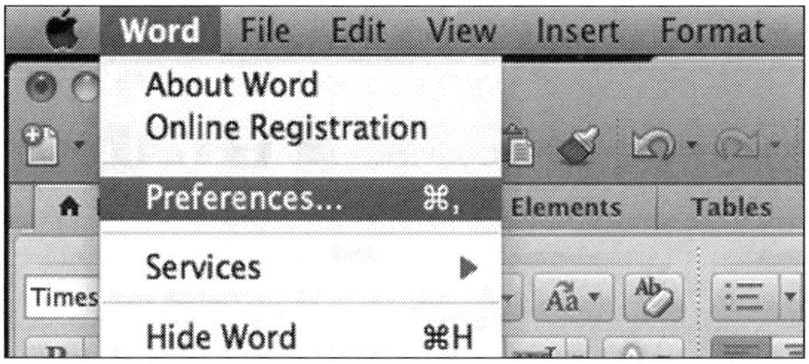

Figure 4.2: Preferences on the Mac version of Word.

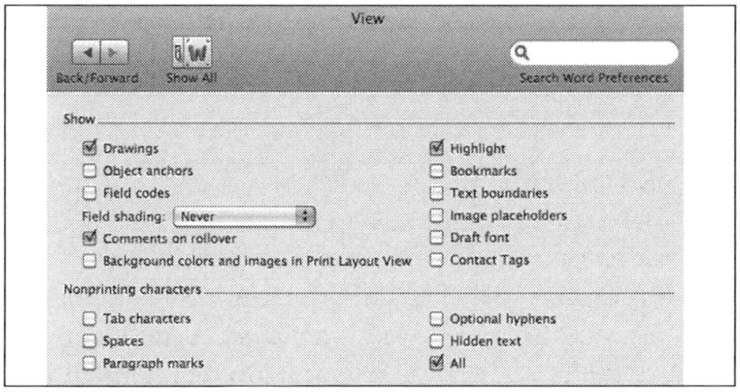

Figure 4.3: "Nonprinting characters" in the View section of Preferences on the Mac Version of Word.

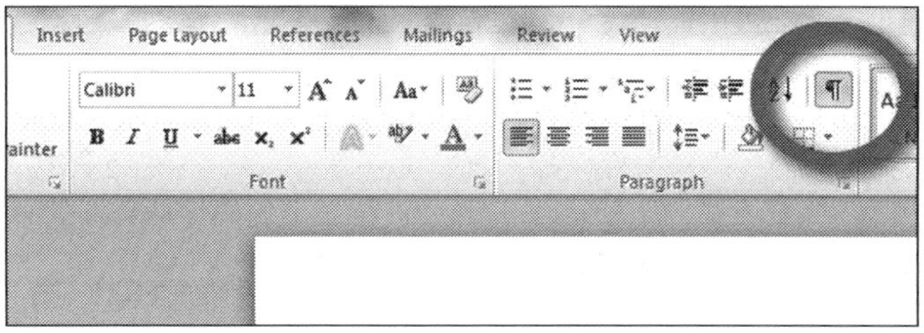

Figure 4.4: On the PC (as well as the Mac), the "Invisible characters" selection is usually on the Home Ribbon.

Fonts

In the Mac version of Microsoft Word, the default font can be changed by going into the Format menu, selecting "Fonts," inputting Times New Roman, and setting the font size at 12 points in the dialogue box. This way, you don't have to keep resetting your fonts.

At the bottom of the Font dialogue box is a button that reads, "Default" (see **Figure 4.5**). Select the "Default" button and another dialogue box will appear, explaining that this change will affect all following documents. Select "Yes" and the smaller dialogue box will disappear. Then select the "OK" button on the bottom of the Font dialogue box and your settings will be saved.

Randomly click in the document to de-select the type.

> *Note:* A "dialogue box" is generally a box that appears in a program where the computer user is having a "conversation" with the computer program or application; in this case, Microsoft Word. By "asking a question," the computer application (app) is going to customize or refine the computer user's desired characteristics and features in an application.

Figure 4.5: Setting the Default Font for all Microsoft Word documents on the PC (Windows). This can be changed as often as the user desires.

Aligning Text, Line Spacing, and Indents

After changing the fonts, let's change the line spacing. Select All (Mac: Command + A; Windows: Control + A). For the Mac, go into the Format menu and select "Paragraph." A dialogue box will appear. Check to see that the "Indents and spacing" tab is selected. Make sure the Alignment reads "Left" (see **Figure 4.6**). To set a 0.5" indent for each paragraph, under the "Indentation" section, go to the "Special" area and select "First line." The default measurement is 0.5". For Windows, click on the Paragraph Bar's little box and follow the directions above (see **Figures 4.7 and 4.8**).

To ensure that the document's line spacing is "double spaced," go to the "Spacing" area and select "Double" under "Line spacing." Once the line spacing has been set at "double spaced," click the OK button on the lower right side of the dialogue box and then randomly click in the document to deselect the text. The document should be roughly one-and-a-half pages.

Since the paragraph indents have been set to 0.5," it is necessary to realign the "Badge" so it aligns with the non-indented parts of each paragraph. Move your cursor to the first letter of each four lines of the "Badge" and press backspace or delete so that the student name, teacher's name, course name, and date align with the 1" paragraph margins, not the 0.5" indents for those paragraphs.

Do the same to the paper's title: delete the indent so the title aligns with the non-indented, one-inch margin of the paragraph and then select "center align" the title.

> *WARNING:* Do not use the tab key or the space bar to "center" text.

Once the first five lines of the paper (Badge and Title) are aligned left, click or highlight the title and click on the "center align" symbol in the menu.

> *Note:* some versions of Microsoft Word defaults are set to 10 points of line spacing between paragraphs. Make sure that

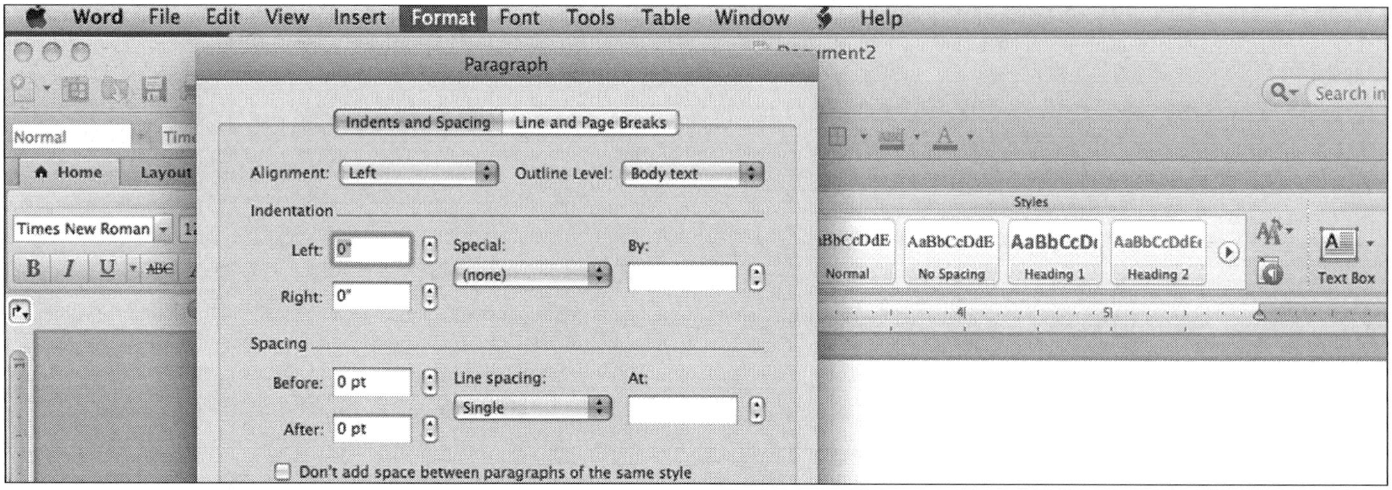

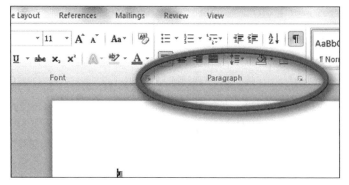

Figure 4.6: The Paragraph Formatting palette can be reached by going into the Format menu on the Mac. The keyboard shortcut to this palettee is "Option + Command + M."

Figure 4.7: The Paragraph Formatting palette can be reached by clicking on the small box in the lower right corner of the Paragraph bar along the Home Ribbon in the Windows version of MS Word.

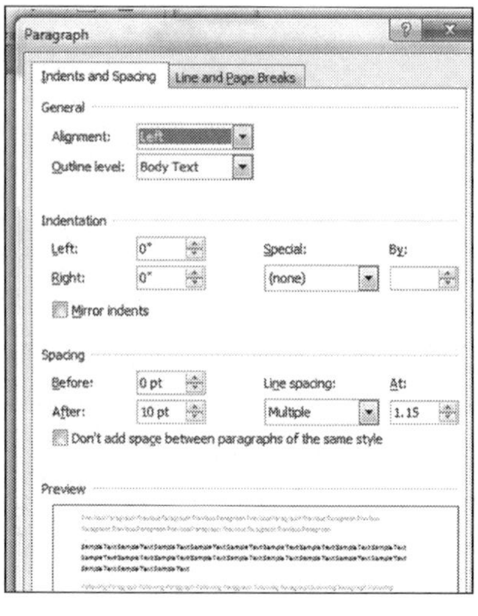

Figure 4.8: The Paragraph Formatting palette in the Windows version of MS Word.

the "Before" and "After" sections read "0 pt" in the area where a numerical value is to be input.

Running Head

On the Mac: Go to the Insert menu and select "Page numbers" (**Figures 4.9** and **4.10**). A dialogue box will appear. Make sure the settings are on "Top of Page (Header)" and the alignment is "Right." Hit OK. A gray number will appear in the upper right corner of the page. It will print black but appears gray, indicating that the number is not part of the "live" or "body" text, which means it will not reflow or move with the rest of the text as you type.

After selecting the OK button on the Page Numbers dialogue box, double-click on the number that appears in the upper right corner. A blue line will appear along the top of the page. In most cases, the cursor will appear on the left side of the page. Select "Align Right" in the Formatting ribbon (**Figure 4.11**) and type your last name. To get out of the "blue lined area," either click on the "Close" button or double-click with your cursor below the blue line.

Screen shots for the Windows platform are on the next page. Although setting up a running head in the Windows version of MS Word is similar to the Mac edition, a shortcut can be used where the user skips the

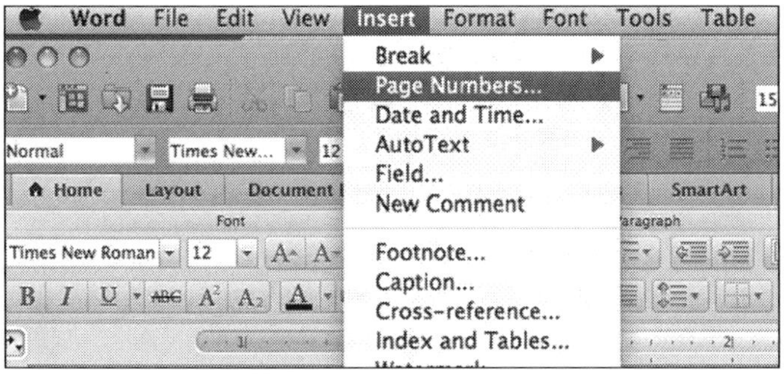

Figure 4.9: On the Mac, page numbers are inserted by going to the Insert menu, selecting "Page numbers..."

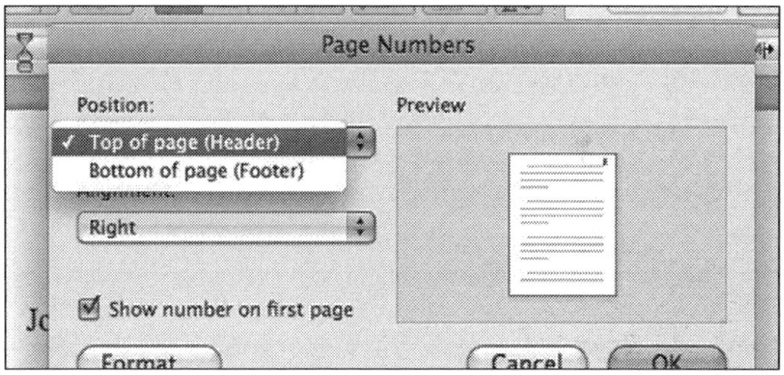

Figure 4.10: On the Mac, for the MLA format, students should select "Top of page (Header) and selecting "Alignment: Right."

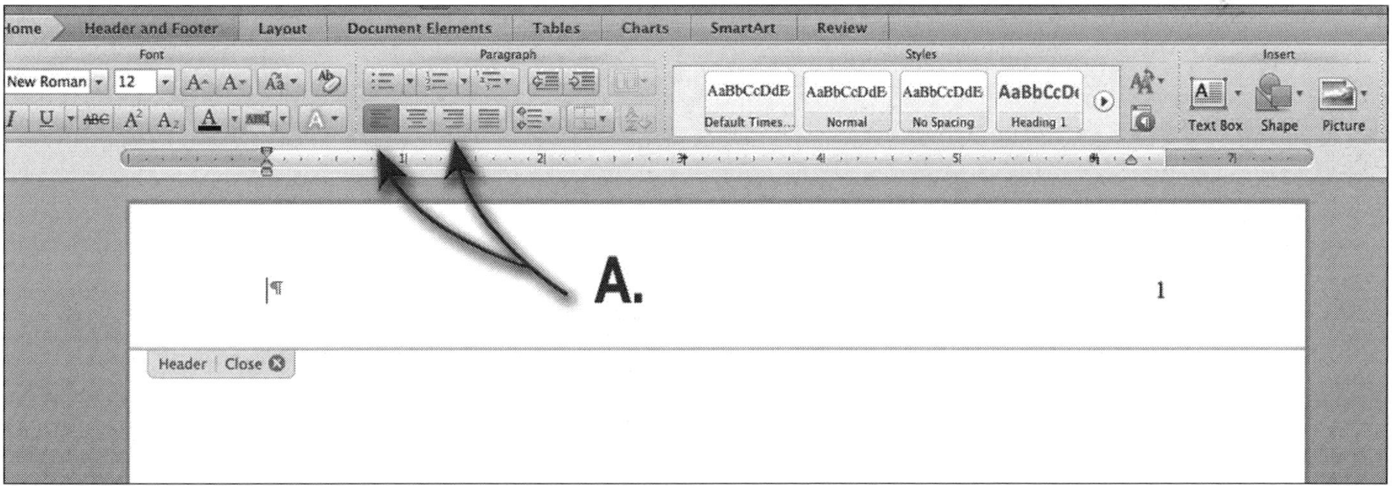

Figure 4.11: A blue line will appear at the top of the page with the computer-generated number in the right corner, indicated by a gray box surrounding the digit. The default setting is "left align." Click on the right-align selection in the toolbar (A.) and type your last name. To get out of this setting, double-click below the blue line.

"Header" option listed in the ribbon, goes directly to the "Page Number" icon (**Figure 4.12**) and sets up the running-header by selecting the Page Number >>Top of Page and selecting the third option in the gallery.

There Is An Easier Way

All of these formatting options are being accomplished on a "work-as-you-go" basis. These formatting options (i.e., font style and size, paragraph line-spacing, indents, etc.) can all be set up in a "Style Sheet" that can be applied to text within an MS Word document. In fact, there are templates that come with Microsoft Word or can be downloaded from Microsoft's Web site specifically for the MLA format.

The purpose of learning how to format a paper from "scratch" is, when it comes time to use Style Sheets, they will be easier for you to edit. Besides, if you ever need to create a newsletter or other printed materials for a club or organization you belong to, learning how to format paragraphs in Microsoft Word is advantageous. Although there are templates for newsletters and such, you may want a more individualized approach. And it's always a plus to remove the "mystery" of anything that has to do with computers: anyone can do this.

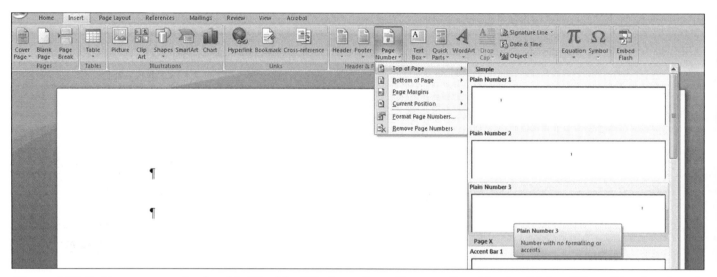

Figure 4.12: Setting up a running head in Word for Windows. Go to "Insert>>Page Number." Select "Top of Page" and a gallery of page number layouts will appear. Select the third one down ("Plain Number 3") with the page number icon indicating it is on the upper right corner. Once the page number appears on the right page, a blue line will appear (similar to the Mac version) and you need to input your last name and then select "right align." After you are finished inputting your last name, you need to change the font of the running head as well as the page number. Select all (Control + A), click on the Home ribbon, and change the font to Times New Roman, 12 pt.

Notes

_____

_____

_____

_____

_____

_____

_____

_____

_____

_____

_____

5 Plagiarism, Avoiding Plagiarism, Citing a Source, and Creating a Works Cited Page

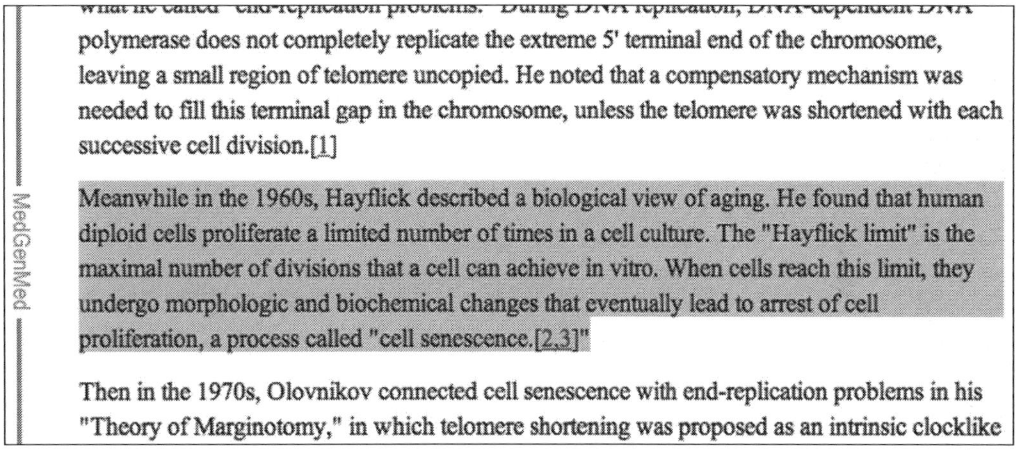
MedGenMed

polymerase does not completely replicate the extreme 5' terminal end of the chromosome, leaving a small region of telomere uncopied. He noted that a compensatory mechanism was needed to fill this terminal gap in the chromosome, unless the telomere was shortened with each successive cell division.[1]

Meanwhile in the 1960s, Hayflick described a biological view of aging. He found that human diploid cells proliferate a limited number of times in a cell culture. The "Hayflick limit" is the maximal number of divisions that a cell can achieve in vitro. When cells reach this limit, they undergo morphologic and biochemical changes that eventually lead to arrest of cell proliferation, a process called "cell senescence.[2,3]"

Then in the 1970s, Olovnikov connected cell senescence with end-replication problems in his "Theory of Marginotomy," in which telomere shortening was proposed as an intrinsic clocklike

Figure 5.1: Web page being high-lighted for "copy-and-paste." If the person doing this simply writes, "According to" and then places the author's name and the name of the publication, there's no foul. Without the attribution, it's plagiarism.

Because of the Internet's wide use and the abuse thereof, most students have been lectured about plagiarism a few dozen times by the time they reach high school. Yes, this is yet another "lecture" on plagiarism.

Plagiarism is defined by the dictionary as, "the practice of taking someone else's work or ideas and passing them off as one's own." There are four general forms of plagiarism:

1. ***Blatant Plagiarism***, where another author's work is presented as the student's own, word-for-word.

2. ***The Plagiarist's Salad***, where multiple authors' works have sentences poached, thrown together, and presented as an original work.

3. ***The Right-Click Thesaurus Plagiarizer***, where the plagiarist copies other authors' sentences, pastes those into Microsoft Word, right-clicks on certain words, selects the suggested alternative words that come from the Thesaurus and changes the original words and presents those ideas as original.

4. ***The Accidental Plagiarist***, where the plagiarist re-writes another author's words and does not give credit for the original idea. Generally, this form of plagiarism is made because the person may not fully understand that plagiarism is not just copying other people's work word-for-word and presenting those ideas as original, but plagiarism is also copying another author's ideas and presenting them as original. There is also the fact that many students are asked to "put it in your own words" by teachers they may have had in earlier grades. Although "putting it in your own words" is preferable, as is paraphrasing, credit must be given to the original source of the idea.

There are other forms of plagiarism that may be combinations of the four listed here, as well as copying work from friends and peers. The allure of plagiarism seems to promise "good grades" with virtually no effort. Or maybe plagiarism spares the student from the "boring" and tedious project from global history. Plagiarism is sort of like a "get rich quick scheme" for the student.

Although many students may not be excited about farming methods along the Nile River in ancient Egypt, these writing projects will develop skills necessary for living in our technologically-based, information-driven society. The ability to understand, analyze and synthesize concepts and ideas is not just limited to the "bookish professions" such as engineering, medicine, law, and teaching; these skills are also related to traditional trades, such as cooking, carpentry, auto-mechanics, plumbing and the rest. Even those who aspire to be famous actors, writers, artists, and musicians need to understand, analyze, and synthesize concepts to contextualize their trade.

Some plagiarism schemes appear to take almost as much time as actually researching and writing the paper itself. If students involved in these plagiarism schemes spent a little extra time, they would avoid the risk of ruining their reputation, plus the time spent dealing with disciplinary measures with teachers, parents/guardians, and school principals. When all is added up, it may actually take less time to research and write a paper than to plagiarize.

As the early 20th Century American humorist, author, swindler and con-artist Wilson Mizner quipped, "If you copy from one author, it's plagiarism. If you copy from two, it's research." Simply reading and reflecting on what was read during research and then putting those thoughts to words is a much better option than plagiarizing.

But keep in mind: most paragraphs in a research paper should have no more than one citation; two if you are presenting opposing views. You want to avoid presenting a pile of quotes that aren't "anchored" into the idea you have to present, thereby giving the appearance that your quotes make up the majority of your paper. Not all ideas need a "citation." General knowledge, such as the French Revolution began in 1789 or that mitosis is cell division, do not need to be cited.

Citing a Source

There are two main ways of citing a source (as well as other variants):

1. *The direct quote*, where the author and his or her credentials are introduced to the reader, and then followed by the author's direct quote. For example:

   According to Jane Smith, a professor of American History at Boston College who specializes in Native American culture, "Native Americans joined the U.S. military during World War Two and their talents were used in developing codes that were impossible to break for the Axis Powers: their native Navajo, Cherokee, and Choctaw languages." (43).

The number in the "parenthetical citation" indicates that this is a page number, which also indicates that this information was taken from a printed book. It is called a "parenthetical citation" because… the reference appears in parenthesis after an author has been quoted or paraphrased. Listing the author's name before the page number in this instance is redundant. A quote from the same author later in the paper would require the author's last name and then the page number in parenthesis.

Also take note of how the quoted author is introduced, and that her area of expertise and her institutional affiliation is identified. It's like introducing a new friend to old friends at a party: give a name and a little background information so the reader gets an idea who you are quoting and why they are being quoted.

2. *The paraphrased quote*, where the author's ideas are paraphrased but still credited. For example:

   According to the Naval History and Heritage Command, the Navajo language, which is unwritten and does not have an alphabet, was used during World War Two to relay classified messages. The U.S. military recruited 200 Navajos whose job was to translate English messages to Navajo and communicate those critical messages to military commanders and back. The Japanese military was unable to "break" or translate those messages. Moreover, the Navajo "code talkers," as they were called, worked faster than coding devices at the time. ("Navajo Code Talkers," n.d.).

Citing a Web Page with No Author Name

The Naval History and Heritage Command is a legitimate Website that gives readers historical accounts of the United States Navy. However, the Naval History and Heritage Command did not provide an author name to its article, entitled, "Navajo Code Talkers: World War II Fact Sheet." Some legitimate Web sites have articles and do not post the author name or date the article was published. Since no author name was provided for the Navajo Code Talkers article, the in-text parenthetical citation should have a reference to the article title, which can be shortened and abbreviated if necessary, and should be easily spotted on the Works Cited page. The "n.d." in the citation is an abbreviation for "no date." If the Naval History and Heritage Command Website provided an author name and date the article was published, the parenthetical citation would look like this: (Brady, 1972).

Sometimes an institution will hire a copywriter to create text for its Website and they don't provide an author name. If a Website does not give the author name, skip the author name and begin your citation with the title of the article. This applies to both your in-text citations and Works Cited entries.

Framing a Quote

Quotes cannot just be thrown together haphazardly; they need to be framed and "set up." Synthesizing and analyzing information, which is a "deeper" and more thorough form of "paraphrasing" and putting things "in your own words," accomplish "framing a quote." Think of "framing" as a type of warning: Here comes a very important quote from an expert on the topic. For example: Dr. Helen Prober, a meteorologist with the National Academy of Sciences, believes "this year's hurricane season is going to be severe." (Prober, 2013).

The Plagiarism Project

Create a new document in Microsoft Word, save and name it properly, and arrange it in the MLA format: your name, teacher name, course name, date, centered title, Times New Roman 12 pt. font, and double-line spacing. The title should be "The Pitfalls of Plagiarism." Write a short essay on plagiarism, at least three paragraphs.

Some things to consider:

- Define plagiarism. Why do students plagiarize? Boring topics? Is everything in life supposed to be entertaining? Is total bliss and happiness what we should all expect in life?

- Is plagiarism wrong? Why is it wrong? Is stealing wrong? What about lying?

- Is plagiarism on the rise? Are there any polls that indicate this? Search News websites and opinion polls

- What do teachers/professors/experts say about plagiarism?

First Paragraph: Define plagiarism and explain why it is dishonest and harmful to both the author and the person committing plagiarism. Is plagiarism more common today than in the past? According to whom? Use an Internet search and seek news stories and polls related to plagiarism.

Second Paragraph: Support your first paragraph by elaborating and going into further detail of news stories and polls that discuss the topic of plagiarism. Find a quote that works and helps make your point.

Third Paragraph: A brief summary and a conclusion: restate what plagiarism is and why it is wrong, but make this statement in a generalized way. Follow this by making a definitive point about plagiarism.

Creating a Works Cited Page: Not a Bibliography

A Works Cited page is different from a bibliography in that it only lists sources that are used in a research paper. The word "Works" indicates that it not only includes books, magazines, newspapers and other printed sources, but may include class lectures, videos, movies, TV shows, Web sites, and other media (as noted earlier).

In contrast, a "bibliography" literally means "book writing," but in the context of how it is used in research papers, it generally is an inclusive list of all published materials used to research a paper, whether those published works are cited or not. Do not conflate "Works Cited" with "Bibliography;" although they are similar, they are not the same. For some reason, some teachers may take this very seriously.

Many Web sites that offer valid information may include at the bottom of the page an MLA entry that readers are encouraged to copy-and-paste, thereby sparing students and researchers the tedious job of typing the entry themselves.

There are also Web sites that generate MLA source entries. Simply type in a search engine like Google or Yahoo! "MLA Works Cited Generator" and a number of these Web sites should appear. Some of the "Works Cited Generators" are not perfect and may introduce problems, such as punctuation. So make sure these generators are doing the job correctly by reviewing the material.

Adopting a Workflow

Although the Works Cited page is the last thing that appears in an MLA formatted paper, it is the first thing that should be finished before writing a paper.

Launch Microsoft Word and appropriately save and name the file (i.e., 06Jones). Input the "badge" (name, teacher name, course name and date). Set all of the necessary formatting (font and size, double-line spacing, etc.). Input the running head (your last name followed by the page number).

After saving this, strike the return/enter key two times and then go into Insert>>Page Break. This will create a fresh page in the document and ensure that the page will always start at the top of the page.

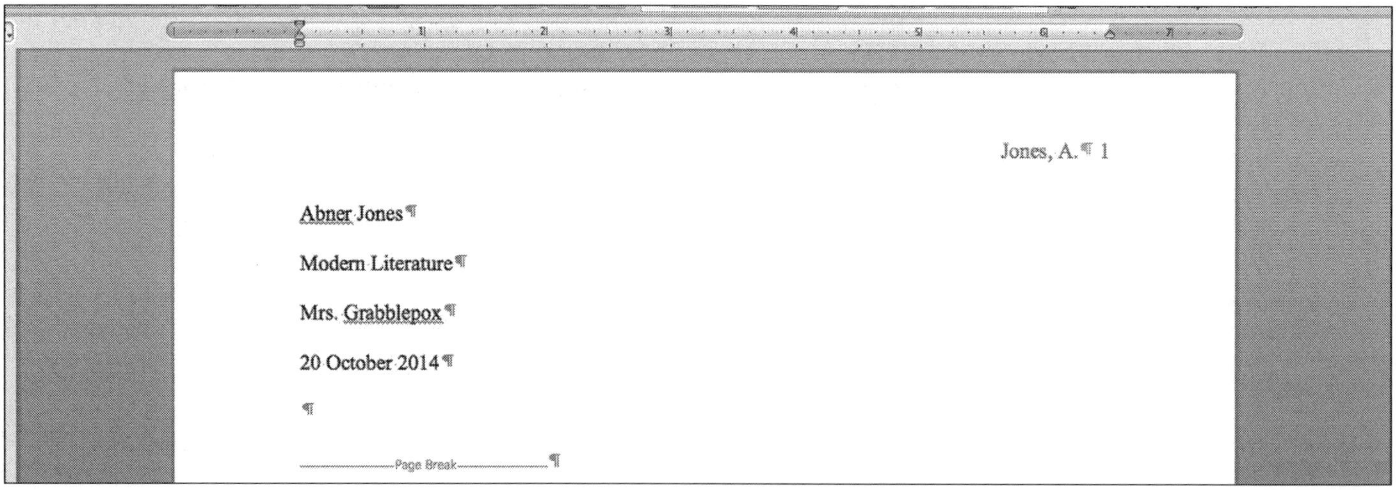

Figure 5.2: Using the "Insert>>Page Break" function to start the Works Cited page first. Since the Works Cited should be worked on as students are doing research, it only makes sense to have an MS Word document open while researching articles on the Internet. Because most people find Works Cited "tedious," it's better to do the Works Cited as you do your research, this way you can keep track of what Web sites you've visited as well as reducing the possibility of misquoting or wrongly attributing a quote to an author or expert. With "non-printing characters" turned on, selecting "Page Break" leaves a non-printing "Page Break" flag that can be easily identified.

Make sure that non-printing characters are turned on. After selecting "Page Break," a non-printing character will appear that demonstrates where the "Page Break" is (see **Figure 5.2**). This can also be deleted just in case.

On the following page, type in Works Cited and center-align the text. Do not underline or bold the text: leave it alone (some people cannot resist underlining and bolding paper titles and sections).

Strike the Return/Enter key. Once a new paragraph marker appears in the center of the page, make sure to set it to align left.

By doing the Works Cited first, you are eliminating one of the more tedious parts of writing a paper and it will also improve the accuracy of your sources. You can keep quotes you intend to use for your paper grouped with your source entries (see **Figure 5.3**). And, when it comes time to use these quotes, they are ready to be copied-and-pasted from the end of the document to where they need placement in your paper. Remember to delete these quotes from the Works Cited page when you are finished with your paper.

Basic Works Cited Entries

We'll start with a book entry. Please note that each media form (Web pages, magazine or newspaper articles, movies, class lectures, etc.) has its own procedure.

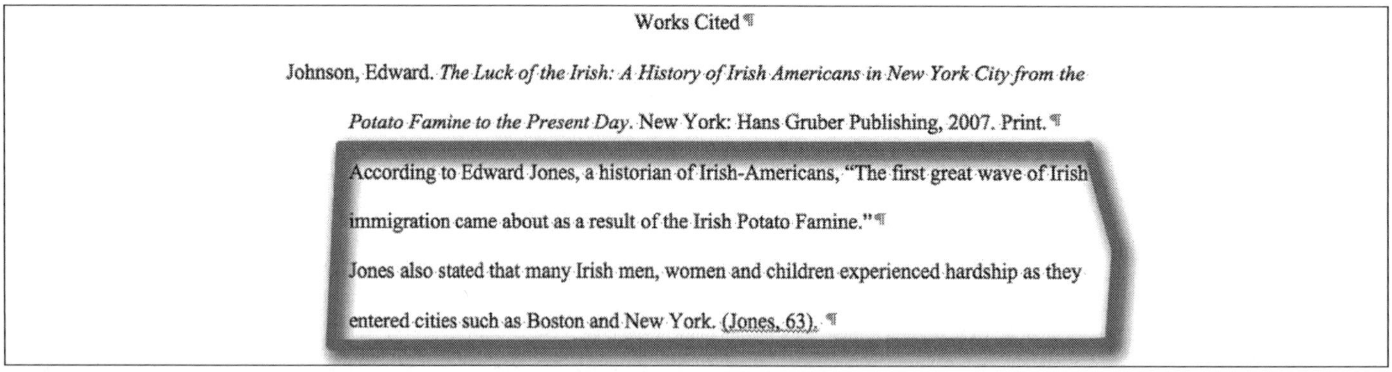

Figure 5.3: By doing the Works Cited page first, you can keep track of useful quotes, thereby avoiding misquoting or misattributing quotes and sources. You will also eliminate the most tedious part of a research paper: instead of having the Works Cited page to finish after writing the main part of the paper, it is already near finished. Be sure to delete the quote from the Works Cited area once you have used it.

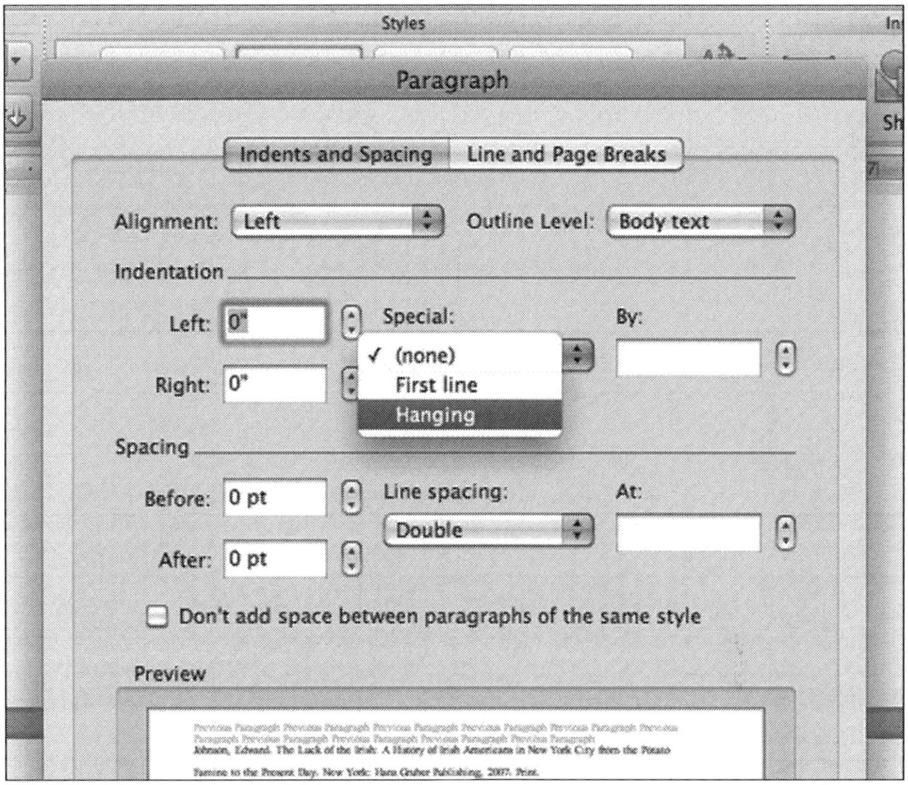

Figure 5.4: The Paragraph Formatting palette on the Mac. Works Cited entries for the MLA format are double-line-spacing with a Hanging indent.

Author last name, author first name. Title of Book (Italicized). City or Country of publication followed by a colon (:), Year of Publication, and then medium (print, eBook, electronic or online book, etc.). Or as follows (this is an example of the "Hanging Indent"):

Johnson, Edward. *The Luck of the Irish: A History of Irish Americans in New York City from the Potato Famine to the Present Day*. New York: Hans Gruber Publishing, 2007. Print.

In your Microsoft Word document, input the above mock Works Cited entry. Once input, highlight only the entry (avoid the Works Cited title). Now go into the Paragraph Formatting palette. Make sure the alignment is set to left. In the Indentation section, look for the area that reads "Special" and make sure it reads "Hanging" by 0.5". Also ensure that the line-spacing is set to double and that "Space After" and "Space Before" both read "0 pt." (see **Figure 5.4**).

> *Note:* A book entry with two authors would have the last name first, comma, and then the author's initial followed by a period: Smith, J. and Johnson, P. A book entry with more than three authors would read: Johnson, E., et al. ("et al." is Latin for "and others").

For a Web page entry, the entry is similar to a book citation. You need to include the author name (if available), the article's title, name of the Website in italics, the name of the publisher (college, school, online magazine, newspaper, etc.), date the Webpage was published, input the word "Web," and then the date you accessed the page. Like so:

Smith, Marvin. "The Truth About the S.S. Minnow." *Harvard Crimson*. Harvard University. 16 April 2004. Web. 30 November 2012.

URLs (Web address links) are no longer required by the MLA. However, you may have a teacher who requires them. If this is the case, then the URL is placed after the date you accessed the page, like so:

Smith, Marvin. "The Truth About the S.S. Minnow." *Harvard Crimson*. Harvard University. 16 April 2004. Web. 30 November 2012. <http://www.monkeygrip-cjlmnop.com/GilligansIsland>

We will address the other types of entries (images, video, class lecture, etc.) later. Works Cited characteristics can also be formatted in Style Sheets, which will also be covered later. To paraphrase Wilson Mizner, an accurate Works Cited page will indicate research, not plagiarism.

6 Computer Vocab and IQ: Parsing Popular Comuter Jargon

Figure 6.1: When the Apple iMac was introduced, there were many people who wondered where the "computer" was. Although earlier versions of the iMac also had the Motherboard, CPU and RAM slots built into the monitor, this design really emphasized Apple's tendency to redefine personal computers (and no, the author did not receive bribe money to praise the Apple computer company). The scanner, keyboard, and mouse are all USB devices.

EVERY PROFESSION has its set of "jargon." Doctors sometimes call the upper leg bone a "femur." And when they say things like, "Fracture of the left femur," for some reason it sounds more grim than saying, "a broken leg."

Lawyers speak in Lawyerese because that's the language they learn in law school. For most people, a cannon is something that appears on a pirate ship that shoots cannonballs. For lawyers, the homophone "canon" is basically a law that sets a standard.

Some teachers, especially those who work in education colleges, speak in a dialect called "edubabble," which every sane teacher knows is nonsense but for some reason, this abomination of the English language is still used today. In fact, many professional jargons are abominations of every day language.

Computer professionals are no different: they have their own jargon. But in this case, their jargon makes sense: usually, the terms are self-explanatory and some of them are in everyday use. You may have even used some of these terms or phrases and have a general understanding of what they mean.

In fact, there have been a number of computer terms used in this book where readers may have a general or vague idea of what they mean, but the specifics are not explained. As well, some of the vocabulary words have not yet been used.

Just as there is vocabulary in subjects like Spanish, French, or English, there is a vocabulary for computers as well. The difference here is that someday you will have to purchase your own computer and/or "smart phone" and knowing the language of computers will improve your "computer IQ" as well as make you a more informed consumer.

Although it is unlikely that you will ever use common high school English vocabulary words like "inexorable" or "conflagration" in "real life," you will ultimately need to understand computer terms especially when you have to deal with IT professionals (the "IT" stands for "Information Technology," by the way), computer salespersons, and other computer people who sometimes appear to be intent on making everyone else feel stupid when in fact, they are just using the language of their profession.

These "Computer Vocab and IQ" sections will appear throughout the book. Although many of the terms may not be specific to this section (Microsoft Word) or other sections in the book, they will be relevant.

Just think: someday in the future, you may be at a party and hear a computer professional complaining that he does not have "enough ram" for his "gooey." Instead of thinking that the person may have issues, you would understand that the person is complaining that he does not have enough Random Access Memory (RAM) to run his graphic user interface (GUI).

Computer Jargon

1. USB (Universal Serial Bus):

_____

_____

_____

2. RAM (Random Access Memory):

_____

_____

_____

3. Storage Memory:

_____

_____

_____

4. General Search in a Program:

_____

_____

5. Select All:

_____

6. Archiving a Web Page:

_____

_____

7. Binary Language:

_____

_____

8. CPU (Central Processing Unit):

_____

_____

9. Motherboard:

_____

_____

10. Application:

_____

_____

_____

7 The Business Letter and Mail Merge

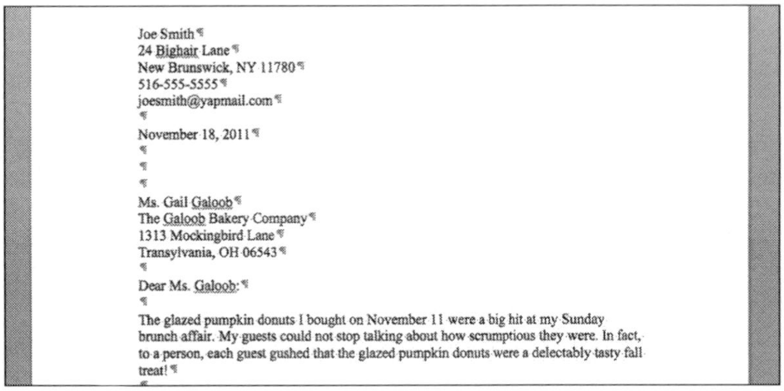

Joe Smith
24 Bighair Lane
New Brunswick, NY 11780
516-555-5555
joesmith@yapmail.com

November 18, 2011

Ms. Gail Galoob
The Galoob Bakery Company
1313 Mockingbird Lane
Transylvania, OH 06543

Dear Ms. Galoob:

The glazed pumpkin donuts I bought on November 11 were a big hit at my Sunday brunch affair. My guests could not stop talking about how scrumptious they were. In fact, to a person, each guest gushed that the glazed pumpkin donuts were a delectably tasty fall treat!

Figure 7.1: A sample of the "block style" business letter. This format is acceptable for both "snail mail" (the U.S. Postal Service) and email.

THERE ARE MANY DIFFERENT FORMATS USED for the business letter. In this exercise, we'll use what is called the "block" format, where every section is aligned left, there are no indents, the document itself has single line spacing and content-wise, is concise and to-the-point. This format is acceptable for both print and email.

There are other forms or styles of business letters that have indents and the letter writer centers his or her contact information along the top of the page. Those are also acceptable. The point of the block form of the business letter is to keep things simple.

Content-wise, some sages say there are four or five different "modes" or "versions" of the business letter. For our purposes here, we'll say there are three. Whatever the motivation behind writing a business letter, whether it's to complain about a product or seek employment, all business letters must be (1) truthful and (2) to the point. Misrepresenting the truth or lying can bring about charges of fraud and this gets even dicier should the letter cross state lines. The goal of a business letter is to be as accurate and concise as possible.

The three types of business letters are (1) the complaint (2) the compliment and (3) the sales-pitch. Keep in mind that whether you are complaining to a company or trying to sell them a thing, you need to be positive and steer clear of insults or ad hominem attacks.

Three Types of Business Letters

1. **The Complaint.** This is when you are writing to express your dissatisfaction with a company, institution, or some other entity that serves or sells to the public. As stated above, what you write must be accurate and truthful otherwise you can be accused of fraud.

    Most reputable businesses, politicians, and/or institutions do not want poor customer relations and should they be at fault for a defective product or unsatisfactory service, a business/person will seek to resolve the problem. Most businesses live by the motto, "The best form of advertising is word-of-mouth." Having customers praise your work is really the most effective form of advertising.

    Now, regarding a complaint to a business, whatever documentation you have (i.e., a receipt, a photo, etc.) that can support your claim should be included as an attachment to the letter. Always make copies of documentation and do not send original items such as receipts, etc.

    For email, scanning a document and saving it as an Adobe Acrobat PDF or jpg image will suffice; for hard copy letters being mailed via

U.S. Postal Service or another delivery service, photocopy or scan and print out a copy of your original receipt (again: Make sure you hold onto your original receipt and documentation).

In both regular U.S. Mail or email, if you have documents that you are sending, be sure to include "enc." at the bottom of the letter, after you sign off with your name. The "enc." should be followed by the name or nature of the document you are enclosing. For example:

Sincerely,

Robert Smith
enc.: Copy of receipt dated August 13, 2011.

2. **The Compliment**. Sometimes people feel compelled to write complimentary letters that praise the products or services of individuals and/or companies. In this case, the same standards of truthfulness and accuracy apply as does the approach: be concise and to-the-point. Depending on who or what the business is, some letter writers may receive promotion items such as tote bags, t-shirts, pens, etc. from the company whereas others may receive a coupon or something along those lines. And sometimes, the individual and/or business may send a thank you letter back. Once again, individuals and businesses that provide services and products generally wish to maintain good relations with their clients and customers.

3. **The Sales Pitch.** There are many different variations of this business letter, but ultimately the letter writer is trying to sell something to another. There's the fund raiser where letter writers try to persuade businesses and individuals to donate to a cause. There's the "Cover Letter," where a prospective employee tries to sell him- or herself to an employer. There's the Straight Sales Pitch, where individuals and companies attempt to sell their goods and services to other individuals and companies. And then there is the dreaded College Essay, which in most cases is just a glamorized business letter dressed up in the essay format where a student tries to persuade a college to admit him or her so the student can accrue a debt that is abouf half of a home mortgage.

The Task: Writing a Business Letter

Create a new folder and name it appropriately in your class folder and in the correct numerical sequence from your previous project (if the last project was named 06Jones, then name the folder "07Jones"). Next, launch Microsoft Word and save this file inside the newly created folder and name it likewise (i.e., "07Jones.docx").

The Premise: You're an aspiring rock star and wish to send ten letters to ten different record companies. You're seeking employment as a rock star and expect the record company will give you a $2 million record advance. An "advance" is a pile of money some record companies give to artists with the hope that future sales will help the company recoup their investment. Many bands over the years, poor and struggling, fall for this money and feel taken advantage of by the time they realize that a record company "advance" is more like a loan. No wonder why so many pop stars seem to embrace socialism and/or Marxian Communism while complaining about capitalist greed in their mansions.

In your letter, you will explain that because you are a sure-fire hit, that you will not be expected to pay back the $2 million advance the record label offers. Because of your talent, instead of getting only five percent of CD and download sales, you expect at least 50% of the sales. Any money that the record label loses will be solely because of the record company's incompetence at marketing and sales. Make sure to be as diplomatic as possible in your letter and do not come across as obnoxious or arrogant.

The letter should be at least two paragraphs and should include all the necessary parts of a business letter (see Sample Letter, next page). As noted above, the line-spacing is single. The top part is the "addresser's contact information." This includes name, street address, city/town, state followed by a zip code (there is no comma between the state and zip code). The "addresser's" phone number and email address should also be included on subsequent lines. The email address is not necessary if you are sending the letter via email.

There should be one line space between the addresser's contact information and the date. The month is always spelled out.

There should be four line spaces between the date and the "addressee's" name and contact information. The addressee's contact information follows the same format as the addresser's name and contact information with slight variations: the addressee's name on one line, the addressee's company name with a "care of" (c/o) placed before it. On the next line, the addressee's company's street address. The line below the street address will be the city/town, followed by the state and zip code. If you used the abbreviation for your state in your contact information, then use the abbreviation for the addressee's state in his or her contact information. You want to be consistent.

It's not necessary to include the addressee's phone number and email; more than likely, the person you are contacting already knows his or her phone number and email address.

Skip one line down and begin your greeting. "Dear" is usually okay, although some people may be uncomfortable with it because "dear" is used by lovers, grandmothers, mothers, fathers, and the like to address someone in an affectionate manner. But "Dear" is also used to address a person one does not know in a polite form.

Make sure that a colon follows the person's name (for example, Dear Mr. Jones:).

Skip another line and begin your letter. Make sure your letter comprises two paragraphs and there is one line space between both paragraphs.

Skip another line to close the letter. A number of sign-offs are "Sincerely," or "Very Truly Yours," or "Sincerely Yours." Make sure each closer has a comma. Skip down four lines and type your name. If you are printing out the letter, be sure to sign your name above where you typed your name. Reminder: there are no indents and everything should be align left.

Below (**Figure** 7.2) is an example of what a block-formatted business letter looks like:

Joe Smith
24 Bighair Lane
New Brunswick, NY 11780
516-555-5555
joesmith@yapmail.com

October 18, 2011

Ms. Gail Galoob
c/o The Galoob Bakery Company
1313 Mockingbird Lane
Transylvania, OH 06543

Dear Ms. Galoob:

The glazed pumpkin donuts I bought on November 11 were a big hit at my Sunday brunch affair. My guests could not stop talking about how scrumptious they were. In fact, to a person, each guest gushed that the glazed pumpkin donuts were a delectably tasty fall treat!

I applaud the hard work of your bakers and the friendly service at the Galoob Bakery Company. I would also be thrilled if my letter joined all the other well-deserved customer letters on the board hanging in your bakery!

Very truly yours,

Joe Smith

Figure 7.2: A block-style business letter.

MS Word: Mail Merge

Once you have written your form letter, it is time to put the "power" of Microsoft Office to good use.

Microsoft Word offers a way of creating a "form letter" and then allowing users to personalize this form letter by automatically inserting different names, addresses and other personalized contact information. Instead of physically cutting-and-pasting or inputting different names and addresses in numerous Word documents, a form letter can be written and then customized for each person the letter writer intends to contact. This is accomplished through a feature called "Mail Merge."

Creating a Mock Database in Excel

We're going to dive into Excel at this point to create some data we'll need to set up the Mail Merge. Launch Microsoft Excel. Select "New Workbook" from either the gallery menu or File>>New>>Workbook and save it into the newly created folder.

> *Note:* In the folder you created, the Microsoft Word document may appear "missing" but that is because you are in Excel. Don't worry, your MS Word documents are still there.

Save the Excel file the same number as the Word and folder number (i.e., 07Jones.xlsx).

Inputting and Basic Functions in Excel

Briefly, Excel is generally a math-based program used to create spreadsheets and other documents. It can be used as a type of database as well. Although mathematical operations are generally associated with Excel, the program is not limited to mathematical operations and can handle a number of other operations, including information-driven Web sites and other visual actions.

You'll notice the "graph paper" quality to Excel. Each one of the boxes in Excel is called a "cell." The horizontal rows are identified by numbers along the left side of the document. Vertical columns are identified by letters along the top. The cursor looks like a white, box-shaped cross. When the cursor is moused-over to a row number, it turns into a rightward arrow. When the cursor is moused over a column letter, it changes into a downward arrow. When you double-click on a cell, the cursor turns into a typing cursor waiting for the user to input text. The cursor also has other variable appearances that will be covered in the Excel chapter.

Cells, rows and columns can be adjusted (widened and narrowed). To adjust the size of a row, move the mouse cursor to the lower part of the row number. The cursor will change into a double-headed arrow cursor. Click and drag with the mouse and move downward. For columns, mouse over to the right of the letter to the right side of the cell. The mouse cursor will convert to a double-headed arrow that points left-to-right. Click and drag the mouse to the right or left to resize the column.

Create the following categories in Excel. **Figure 7.3** demonstrates how to set up the Excel file. But just in case, the column and row number appear in parenthesis after each category:

Mr./Mrs. (A1), Last Name (B1), First Name (C1), Company (D1), Street Address (E1), City/Town (F1), State (G1), and Zip Code (H1). After inputting these "Column Heads," make up ten record companies and record executives including their contact information (see **Figure 7.3**). After your list is completed, bold the category sections by selecting the "1" in the row and then clicking on the "B" (bold) icon in the Home Ribbon.

If you can't make up your own contact information, feel free to use the information provided in **Figure 7.3**. Once you have created the ten contacts and their information, save and close the Excel file.

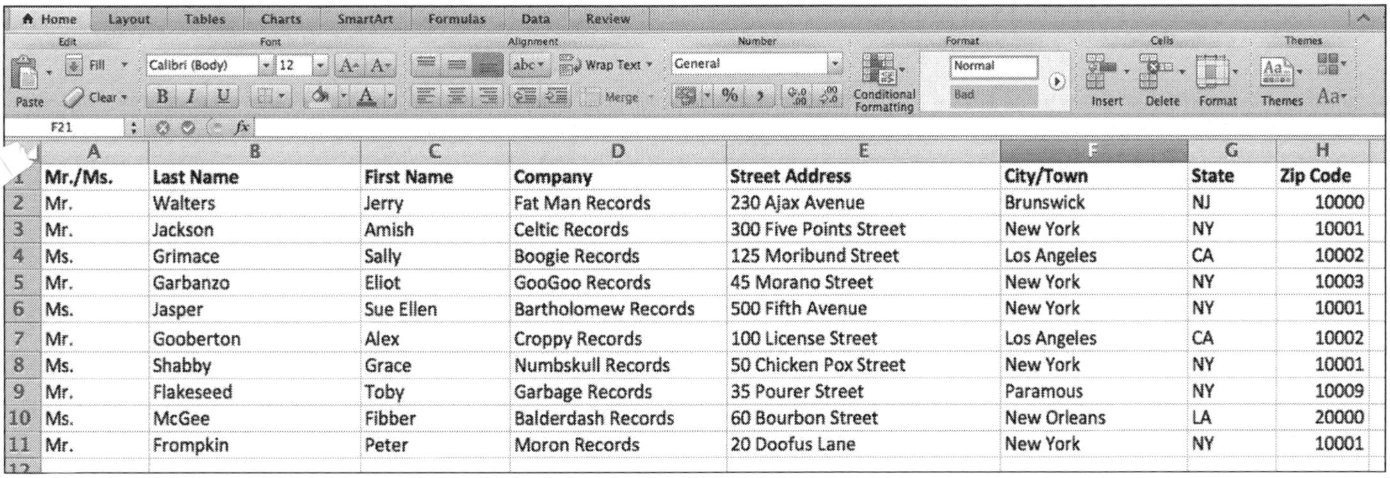

	A	B	C	D	E	F	G	H
1	Mr./Ms.	Last Name	First Name	Company	Street Address	City/Town	State	Zip Code
2	Mr.	Walters	Jerry	Fat Man Records	230 Ajax Avenue	Brunswick	NJ	10000
3	Mr.	Jackson	Amish	Celtic Records	300 Five Points Street	New York	NY	10001
4	Ms.	Grimace	Sally	Boogie Records	125 Moribund Street	Los Angeles	CA	10002
5	Mr.	Garbanzo	Eliot	GooGoo Records	45 Morano Street	New York	NY	10003
6	Ms.	Jasper	Sue Ellen	Bartholomew Records	500 Fifth Avenue	New York	NY	10001
7	Mr.	Gooberton	Alex	Croppy Records	100 License Street	Los Angeles	CA	10002
8	Ms.	Shabby	Grace	Numbskull Records	50 Chicken Pox Street	New York	NY	10001
9	Mr.	Flakeseed	Toby	Garbage Records	35 Pourer Street	Paramous	NY	10009
10	Ms.	McGee	Fibber	Balderdash Records	60 Bourbon Street	New Orleans	LA	20000
11	Mr.	Frompkin	Peter	Moron Records	20 Doofus Lane	New York	NY	10001

Figure 7.3: Inputting contact information into Excel.

Note: Mail Merge works with other programs such as Outlook Express and Address Book (on the Mac).

Onto the Mail Merge: Mac OS

Using Mail Merge on the Mac is fairly different than how it works in Windows. The section describing how to engage Mail Merge in Windows follows this section. So feel free to skip this section if you're using Windows.

Open your letter in Microsoft Word (if it isn't open already). Re-save the letter, keeping the number and your last name intact but adding "_MailMerge" after it. Once you've imported data from other programs, Microsoft Word will constantly seek out that information each time you relaunch that file, so it is a good idea to keep one version of the letter "unfettered." In total, you will have three separate Microsoft Word files when this project is finished.

Once you have re-saved the file, go to the Tools menu (Mac) and select Mail Merge Manager (**Figure 7.4**). In Windows, select the Mailings tab and then click on Start Mail Merge (**Figure 7.5**). In the Mail Merge palette, there will be six sections: (1.) Select Document Type (2.) Select Recipients List (3.) Insert Placeholders (4.) Filter Recipients (5.) Preview Results and (6) Complete Merge.

In the Mail Merge palette, select "Create New" and click "Form Sheet." Now select "Get List: Open Data Source" and navigate to the folder where your Excel file

was saved. The column categories from your Excel document (i.e., Last Name, First Name, Address, etc.) will be listed in the Contacts (go to Insert Placeholders).

Note: After selecting your Excel file, you may get a warning from MS Word that claims it could be a "security risk." Choose "OK". You may get this message again should you close the document and open it again.

Go into the Insert Placeholders area (**Figure 7.5**). Click and drag the categories into their corresponding area on your business letter (the addressee's contact information). For example, the first category from the Excel file is listed a "Last_Name." Click and drag that into the area where addressee's last name is (make sure you delete the last name of the contact who was input into the Word document). The person's name should now look like this: Ms. Gail «Last_Name». Make sure you input a space between the first name and the last (spacebar).

Now click and drag the "First_Name" from the Placeholders area of the Mail Merge palette. It should look like this: «First_Name» «Last_Name» (See **Figure 7.6**). Now replace the rest of the categories. Take note of the scroll bars at the top and bottom of the Placeholders area.

Because the street address appears on the same line as the state and zip code, be sure to input a comma between the city/town and state and to input a space (spacebar) between the state and the zip code.

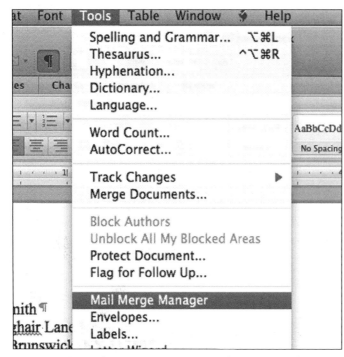

Figure 7.4: Mail Merge Manager on the Mac. In the Windows version, there's a Mailings tab.

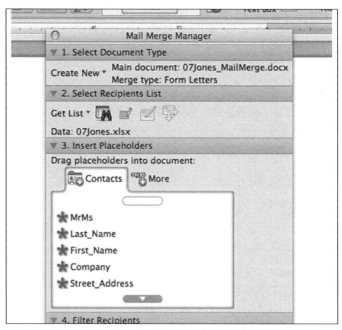

Figure 7.5: Insert Placeholders in the Mail Merge Manager palette on the Mac. The "contacts" are directly imported in once the file has been imported in the "Select Recipients" list.

Now place your cursor to the area where it begins with "Dear" in your letter. Delete "Mr." or "Mrs." and click-and-drag "Mr./Ms." from the Placeholders area of the palette. Do likewise with the First Name and Last Name. Make sure you leave the colon.

When you are finished dragging and dropping all of the information, it should look like the text depicted in **Figure 7.6.**

In the (4.) Filter Recipients, you could eliminate an entry or part of an entry, but let's skip over that.

In the (5.) Preview results, you can look at each entry to ensure accuracy. We'll skip this part as well.

In the (6.) Complete Merge area of the Mail Merge palette, this is where the "action" takes place. You have three choices along the bottom of that section of the palette: (1) Merge to Printer, for print jobs (2) Merge to New Document (this is what we'll be doing for this project) and (3) Generate email messages.

Select "Merge to New Document." A new document with multiple pages will appear. Word will automatically create a document entitled "FormLetters." Be sure to save this file in the job folder and name it the same number as the other files while leaving "FormLetters" in tact. In our example, since we had 10 contacts from our Excel document, there will be 10 pages, each with a "Section Break" appearing at the bottom of the page (a "section break" is similar to a "page break").

To view the document and its section pages on the Mac, click on the toolbar icon "Show or hide Sidebar" or go to View>>Sidebar>>Thumbnail pane.

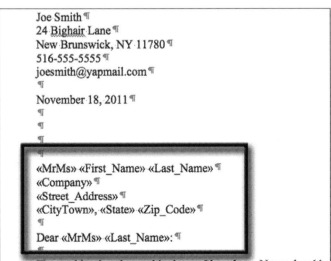

Figure 7.6: Once the placeholders have been dragged and dropped from the Insert Placeholders section of the Mail Merge palette, it will create a section based on the information from the Excel file. Each category will be identified by angle brackets or "carrots." («,»).

Using Mail Merge in Windows

Re-save the letter, keeping the number and your last name intact but adding "_MailMerge" after it. With the newly renamed business letter open, click on the Mailings tab, look for the Select Recipients icon. Click on the down-arrow and select, "Use Existing List" (see **Figure 7.7**). A dialog box will appear.

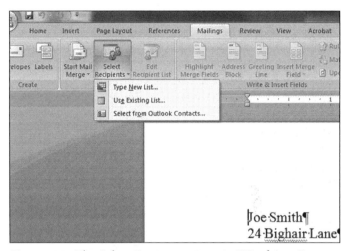

Figure 7.7: The Select Recipients icon in Windows. Be sure to select "Use Existing List..." and navigate to your Excel file in your job folder.

Navigate to the Excel "database" you created and select it. After you select the Excel file, another dialog box entitled "Select Table" will appear. Make sure you select "Sheet1$" and that the check-off box in front of "First row of data contains column headers" is selected (see **Figure 7.8**). Now select "OK."

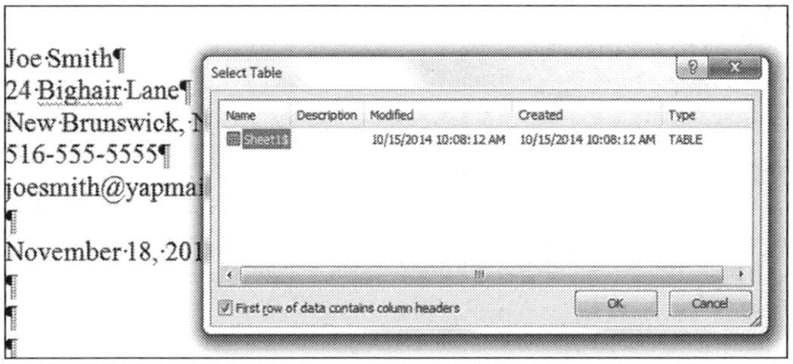

Figure 7.8: Be sure to select Sheet1$ when the Select Table dialog box appears.

Next, locate the Insert Merge Field icon in the Mailings ribbon. Highlight the "Mr." or "Ms." in the addressee's name in the letter. Now click on the down-arrow below the Insert Merge Field icon and select "Mr./Ms" (see **Figure 7.9**). The placeholder text ‹‹Mr./Ms.›› should appear. Follow the same steps for the remaining parts of the addressee's contact information (i.e., First Name, Last Name, Company Name, Street Address, City, State and Zip Code).

Figure 7.9: The Insert Merge Field icon. Be sure to click on the down-arrow and select the appropriate placeholder text as it corresponds to each area in the addressee's contact information.

Go to the salutation (example, "Dear Mr. Jones") and select the "Mr." or "Ms." text. Delete that and then go back to the Insert Merge Field icon's down-arrow, select "Mr./Ms." Now delete the last name but leave the colon. Next, go back to the Insert Merge Field icon's down arrow and select "Last Name." Make sure there is a space between ‹‹Mr./Mrs.›› and ‹‹Last Name››.

Once you have inserted the placeholder text, go back to the Mailings ribbon and look for the "Finish & Merge" icon. Click on the down-arrow and select "Edit Individual Documents" (see **Figure 7.10**).

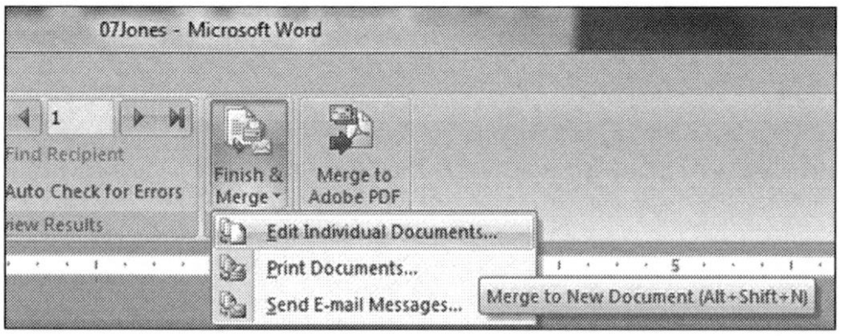

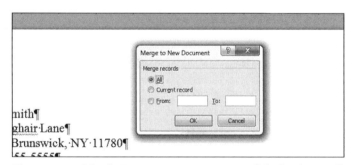

Figure 7.10: The Finish & Merge icon. Be sure to select "Edit Individual Documents." This will create a new Word file that you have to re-name and save.

A dialog box entitled "Merge to New Document" will appear (see **Figure 7.11**). Make sure the radial button is selected to "All" and then click "OK." A new document will appear. There should be ten pages within the document, each the same letter addressed to the different people from your Excel file. Go to "Save As" and save the file "07JonesMERGE" in the job folder you created at the beginning of this project.

Figure 7.11: The "Merge to New Document" dialog box will appear. Be sure to click on "All."

Notes

_____

_____

_____

_____

_____

8 The MLA Research Paper: Pregame Show

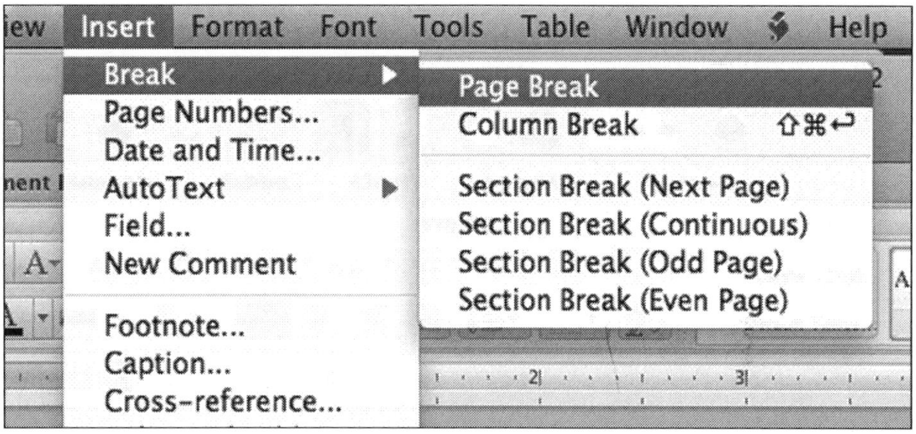

Figure 8.1: Nothing says "Power User" like using the Page Break.

THERE ARE GENERALLY TWO TYPES of research papers: (1) Explanatory or "expository", where the author is explaining a topic and (2) Argumentative, where the author is taking a position with regards to a topic.

Some say there is a third type of paper, sometimes called "analytical," where the author analyzes a thing and presents a conclusion, but "analytical" can also apply to both the "argumentative" and "explanatory" types of papers. In fact, the "analytical" aspect should be applied to both "explanatory" and "argumentative" papers. When teachers use "analyze" or "analytical," they want you to organize information, relate, compare, or contrast that information with other opinions, discuss what is factual and make inferences or hypotheses (conclusions based on the evidence). A solid paper not only "analyzes," but it also relays "critical thinking."

Sometimes, when a teacher or professor uses the phrase, "critical thinking," it can mean, "I want you to think the way I do and you must agree with me or get a bad grade." But true "critical thinking" is (1) being aware of your own biases, (2) being aware of the source's biases, (3) researching a topic thoroughly, (4) seeking out opposing opinions, (5) applying the "Devil's Advocate theory" to your own conclusions and trying to prove yourself false, and (6) presenting a conclusion that is consistent with the facts and other components presented in a paper.

One of the most difficult problems in writing a research paper is where and how to start. The simple answer is "research." And then more "research." If you research your project thoroughly, writing the paper will be much easier.

Another challenge with research papers is that most people generally do not like to do them even if they are enthusiastic about the subject. Yet for roughly eight years, teachers and professors are going to require research papers and some courses in college are based primarily on the ability to write a solid paper. No one is "born" with a talent to write research papers; researching and then writing a paper are skills that need to be developed.

Preparing for a Research Paper

As noted earlier, the "Works Cited" page is generally the last page to appear in an MLA formatted paper. It is the first thing the author should do when writing a paper: keep track of your sources (pages 17—18).

Other sources that can be used in a research paper are class or campus lectures given by teachers, visiting speakers and experts, and other professionals. Movies and television can also be used. If you're writing a research paper that is related to a lecture or classroom discussion presented by a teacher or professor, keep accurate notes and be sure to date those notes.

Organizing Sources (Works Cited)

Once it has been established that Websites you are using are legitimate, entries can be made in the "Notes" document. Eventually, entries appearing on the "Works Cited" page needs to be alphabetized and put into order.

A few things: some Websites that are legitimate do not necessarily list an author name. When the author name is not available, skip it and begin the entry with the article title. Article titles are in quotes; names of publications (magazine titles, newspapers, etc.) are italicized.

The MLA format requires two dates: the first date is the publishing date, the second date is the day you visited the Web site. If the article you have chosen does not have the date the article was posted, write the abbreviation, n.d. for "no date."

In the MLA format, is not necessary to use the uniform resource locator (URL) or Web address. However, a teacher or professor may require including the URL in the entry. Therefore, angle brackets (<, >) should surround the Web address if a student decides to use it. Some URLs may take up more than one line of text; don't fuss if the URL exceeds one line and flows into the next.

The following are two examples of how Web citations should look in the Works Cited page of an MLA paper:

Author Last name, Author first name. "Title of Article." (in quotes, period inside quotes). Sponsor or publisher of Web site. Date article was posted (use "n.p." if no date is available). Type of publication: in this case, "Web." Date you were at the Website. URL in angle brackets: <http://www.parrotsrule.com>

Or for example:

Pyle, Artimus. "Drumming for Lynyrd Skynyrd." Rock-n-Roll History. 20 October 2007. Web. 12 May 2013. <http:www.rocknrollhistory.com/pyle_skynyrd.html>

Note: in some versions of Microsoft Word, the angle brackets might "disappear" if there is no space between the URL and the brackets and the return/enter key or space bar is pressed. This is because of the "AutoFormat" feature that is a default setting in many versions of Microsoft Word. This can be undone by simply going into the Edit menu and selecting "Undo AutoFormat" or pressing "Command + Z" on the Mac or "Control + Z" on a Windows keyboard.

Some Websites anticipate that researchers will use their information and may post the MLA citation (as well as other formats, such as APA, Chicago, etc.) at the bottom of the article. In this case, copy-and-paste the information into the Word document. When the copied text appears in the Word document, an icon of a clipboard will appear at the end of the copied text that has an upside-down triangle on the right (see **Figure 8.2**): mouse over the arrow and select "Match destination formatting" so the text conforms to the Times New Roman, 12 point and double line spacing. Always check to see if the citation information provided by the Website is up-to-date with the MLA format; the MLA format has updates and changes to its form.

There are also online citation generators, such as EasyBib (http://www.easybib.com/) or Citation Machine (http://www.citationmachine.net/). These are very helpful and self-explanatory.

The Hanging Indent

Works Cited entries, that is the list of sources that were used for a paper, have double line spacing and have what is called a "Hanging Indent." Instead of the first line being indented in a paragraph, the first line extends to the paper's margins and any lines that follow are indented .5" beneath the first line.

To format the entries for a Works Cited page in Microsoft Word, make sure the desired text is highlighted; go into the Paragraph formatting palette and make sure that it reads "Indents and Spacing" along the top. In the

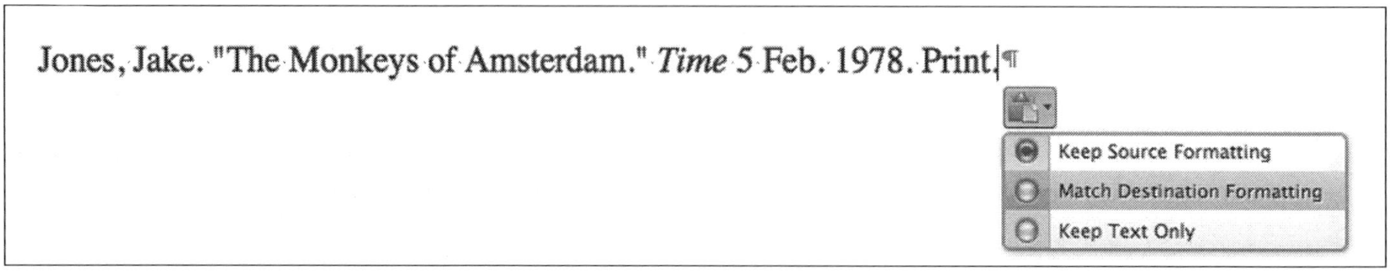

Jones, Jake. "The Monkeys of Amsterdam." *Time* 5 Feb. 1978. Print.

Keep Source Formatting
Match Destination Formatting
Keep Text Only

Figure 8.2: Copying-and-pasting text into a Word document; a clipboard icon will appear at the end of the chunk of text being pasted. Click on the inverted triangle next to the clipboard and select "Match Destination Formatting" to allow the copied text to conform to the formatted text set in the Word document.

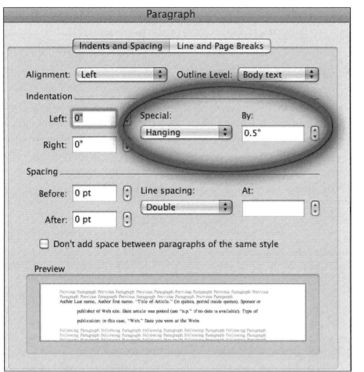

Figure 8.3: Setting up a Hanging Indent in the Paragraph formatting palette. Remember to highlight the appropriate text when formatting.

"Indentation" section, go to the middle area and look for "Special:" and then select "Hanging." Make sure it reads "by 0.5". Be sure that the "Line Spacing:" area in the "Spacing" section of the palette is set at "Double." A preview of what the paragraph looks like will appear in the window below (see **Figure 8.3**).

> *Note:* Any quotes or notes that you input after this formatting will have the hanging indent. If it is bothersome, highlight the quote/text, go to the Paragraph palette and select "(none)" in Indentation section.

Evaluating and Assessing a Website

One of the great things about the Internet is the ability to reach information within seconds. And just as this is a blessing, it is also a curse: for every legitimate Website on the Internet, there may be hundreds addressing the same subject that are specious, biased, or intellectually dishonest. The key word here is "legitimate." What does it take for a Website to be valid?

> *Note:* just because a Website has a ".edu" or a ".org," it does not mean that Website is automatically "legitimate." There are numerous groups that can be considered "extreme" that also use the ".edu" or

".org" domains. Also, just because a person has a "Dr." in front of his or her name or a "Ph.D." after, it does not mean he or she is necessarily sober or accurate.

Biases and Such

Regarding politics, unless the source is truly "extreme right wing" or "hardcore left wing," avoid using strong labels for opposing points of view. "Conservative," "right-leaning," "progressive," and "left-leaning" are preferable to the ad hominem labels one sees all over the Internet. If you are describing a group that is "extreme," make sure that such a statement can be proven true; otherwise you leave yourself open to a bottomless philosophical pit regarding what defines "extreme." Many times, Democrats and Liberals will describe Republicans and Conservatives as "extreme" (and vice-versa) when in reality, such labeling is just political posturing.

Also, currently there is a "media war" between new forms of news and information (the Internet, cable news, etc.) and older, more traditional sources, such as network television news (ABC, CBS, NBC, and Fox affiliated stations), newspapers (*The New York Times*, the *Washington Post*, etc.) and magazines (*Time Magazine, Business Week*, etc.). Take note how critics of FOX News claim it "lies" and does not broadcast the truth, just as critics of old media say the same about ABC, CBS, NBC and so on. Both sides of this media battle present similar arguments about one another. Good luck sorting through it. Your job is not to take sides and call media personalities "liars;" your job is to assess if the information is accurate and reliable.

And beware: there are many "fact checker" websites on the Web that claim to be neutral yet push an agenda as well. The "fact" is, even the "fact checkers" facts need to be checked for accuracy. There are a number of groups that pretend to be "objective" but spend a great deal of time pushing their own agenda through this spurious "objectivity."

Regarding sources and authors, check the author's credentials: an author who has an Ed.D. in education or Ph.D. in English may not be the most qualified person to be writing an article on quantum physics or history; conversely, a person with a masters degree in history or math may be qualified to write about quantum physics. Find out "what" qualifies the author. Academic credentials are generally good indicators, but like all professions, there are fair shares of "professionals" who frequently publish articles on the Internet; the education field has its share of "quacks" like every other profession. Always verify the author's credentials and see where else he or she has been published.

When reading an article where the author quotes another author or expert, if possible, look up and read the article that is being referenced. Like the allegedly "wise" fact-checkers, sometimes authors misquote or take their sources out of context.

Searching a Web Page

Web pages that use text can be searched, like any other document on a computer. The "universal" search command on Macs is, "Command + F"; on Windows, it's "Control + F." Some articles may be very long but contain information that is necessary for your paper. Instead of reading a 5000-word essay or investigation, a word search can be used to bring the researcher to the critical information. In both Safari (the Web browser for the Mac) and Internet Explorer (the Web browser for the PC), the "Find" option is located in the "Edit" menu. A search bar will appear on the browser (see **Figure 8.4**) and allow you to input text for a search.

Archiving a Web Page

Once it has been established that the Website is legitimate and because Web pages can be updated, it's a good idea to printout or archive the source. To archive a Web page, go to the browser's File menu, scroll down to "Save As," and save the Web page to the job folder you created. (see **Figure 8.5**). On the Mac, the file's icon will have a Safari logo; on Windows systems, a folder will be created and inside that folder will be the Web page (HTML file) as well as any images used on that Web page.

> *Caution:* Be sure to have your anti-virus software running and to verify the Web site before archiving it.

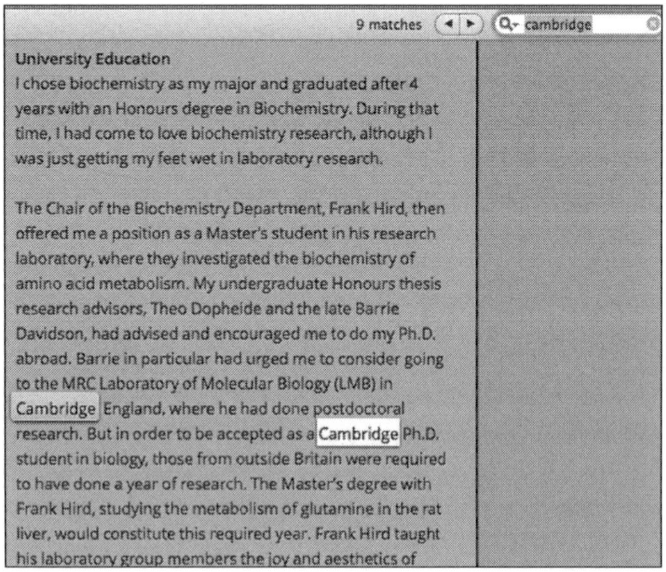

Figure 8.4: A word search can be conducted on any Web page that has text; Command + F on the Mac or Control + F in Windows.

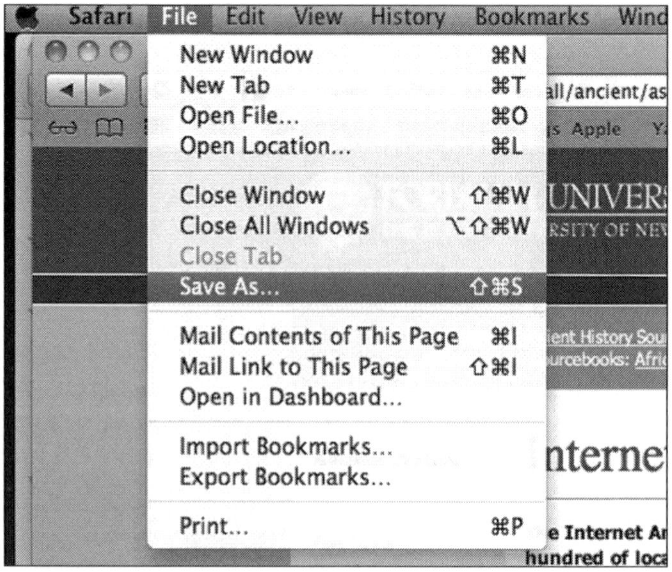

Figure 8.5: "Archiving a Web page" sounds so "computer-y." Web pages can be saved to your hard drive or network drive like any other program files, like Word or Excel.

9 MLA Formatting: The Expository Research Paper

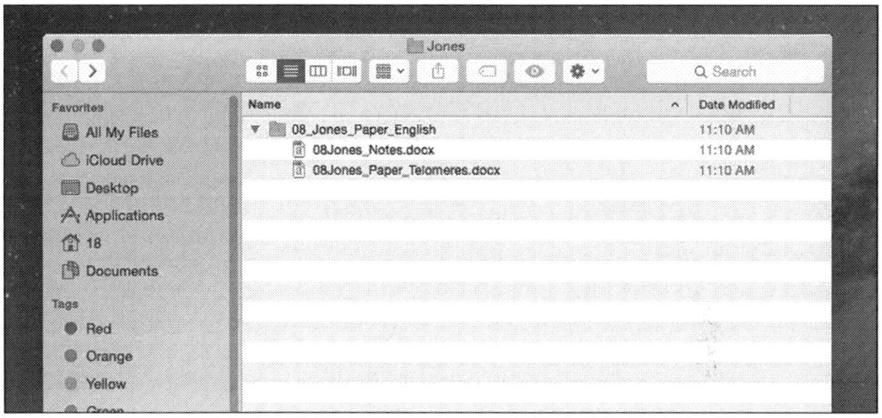

Figure 9.1: Whenever you're writing a research paper, it's a good practice to have a notes file for copying-and-pasting references, inputting quotes that back up your thoughts, and keeping track of your sources.

THIS PROJECT WILL CONSTRUCT a five-paragraph expository scientific research paper utilizing Internet sources. It is going to examine mythical, religious, and scientific sources and explain the possibility of "immortality" and/or human longevity: can a person live forever, or for at least a few centuries? Just as flight was once thought impossible and is now possible, is science and technology once again turning the impossible into the possible?

Navigate to your class folder, open it and look at the "directory" in the "List" mode. Your previous class exercises should be visible and in numerical order (the last file you worked on should be at the bottom). Create a new folder in your class folder so it is among the existing Microsoft Word documents. Name the new folder with the next number in sequence; if your last file was 07Jones, then the new folder should be named "08Jones_Paper" (of course, "Jones" is just an example last name, use your last name).

Close the folders and launch Microsoft Word. You're going to need two Microsoft Word documents for this project: the first document should be named "08Jones_Notes" and the second document should be named, "08Jones_Paper."

The first document, "08Jones_Notes," is going to be used to keep track of the information you gather. Once you've decided that a Website is legitimate and is offering valid information that can be used for your research, copy-and-paste the author's name, the article's title, the Website's publisher, the date the article was posted and the date you were there. You should also copy-and-paste the Website's uniform resource locator (URL), the Web address that usually starts with http://www. Make sure you record the date in your "Notes" file. If there are "critical quotes" or information that you wish to paraphrase, be sure to copy that information beneath the author's name and publication information.

Formatting and Pre-writing

For the "Notes" document, make sure the font is Times New Roman 12 pt., it is double-line spaced, and in the paragraphs palette. In the "Paper" document, put your name, teacher's name, course name, and date, and input the title, "Science and Legend: The Quest for Immortality or Longevity Continues," the paper's topic. Finally, archive or save the Web pages into your project folder on your drive (e.g., 08Jones_Paper).

Questions and Brainstorming: write short answers to the questions and observations.

1. There is the impression that science is all "hard facts" and there is no room for myth, culture, or religion in scientific circles. Yet what was once

thought to be myth and impossible, science and technology has turned into reality. The ancients dreamed of conquering diseases and fancied ideas such as flight, as well as human immortality and human longevity. Today, thanks mainly to science, some diseases have been conquered and flight is now a reality. Is immortality or leading an extraordinarily long life far behind?

2. Any ancient stories or ideas that are related to immortality? What about human longevity? Any popular movies or stories deal with human immortality/longevity today or recently?

Human Longevity/Immortality:

_____

_____

_____

Human Immortality (Bible? Movies? Legends?):

_____

_____

_____

Human longevity (Bible? Movies? Legends?):

_____

_____

_____

3. Scientific discovery: Identify mitosis. What does mitosis have to do with aging? (Internet search engine, Google or Bing).

_____

_____

_____

4. What is the "Hayflick Limit?" (Internet search engine, Google or Bing).

_____

_____

_____

5. Identify telomeres. What role do telomeres play during mitosis? Who discovered the structure and function of telomeres?

"The 2009 Nobel Prize in Physiology or Medicine - Speed Read". Nobelprize.org. Nobel Media. 12 May 2014. Web. 25 Aug 2014. http://www.nobelprize.org/nobel_prizes/medicine/laureates/2009/speedread.html

6. Identify telomerase. What is it, and what does it have to do with aging?

_____

_____

_____

_____

_____

_____

7. Experiments with Telomerase: There are two prominent experiments conducted by Dr. Ronald DePinho, president of the University of Texas MD Anderson Cancer Center and a renowned expert in the field of telomerase therapy.

_____

_____

_____

_____

_____

_____

First Experiment: Callaway, Ewen. "Telomerase reverses ageing process." *Nature*. 28 November 2010. Web. 14 June 2014. http://www.nature.com/news/2010/101128/full/news.2010.635.html

The second experiment: "Blocking Telomerase Kills Cancer Cells but Provokes Resistance, Progression." MD Anderson Cancer Center, University of Texas. 20 February 2012. Web. 16 May 2013. http://www.mdanderson.org/newsroom/news-releases/2012/blocking-telomerase-kills-cancer-cells-but-provokes-resistance-progression.html

Other Useful Link(s):

"Telomeres, Telomerase, and Tumorigenesis—A Review." By Lin Kah Wai, Fellow, Lviv National Medical University, Lviv, Ukraine http://www.ncbi.nlm.nih.gov/pmc/articles/PMC1435592/

Notes

Explain Telomeres and Telomerase

_____
_____
_____
_____
_____

Identify a nucleotide:

_____

What do scientists think Telomeres and telomerase can do for humanity?

_____
_____
_____
_____

Do telomeres and telomerase show promise in the fight against cancer? What about aging?

_____
_____
_____
_____
_____
_____
_____
_____

10 Expository Writing: Grammar, Transitions, Prepositions, and Some Writing Tips

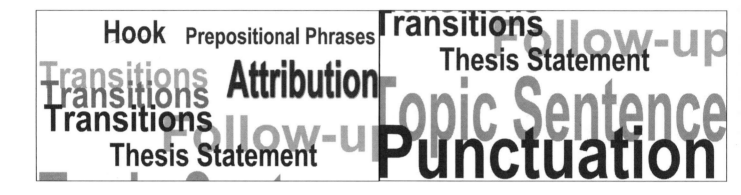

IN MANY CASES, SCIENTIFIC WRITING can be dry and boring, especially in the "expository" (explanatory) area. Most students tend to get focused on the "facts" and/or "observations" made by scientists and if the subject area is difficult, students may get "bogged down" in the details. Sometimes a literary, musical, or artistic approach to science may help make a science paper easier to understand.

When tackling a scientific topic, it's a good idea to see if the discovery or invention relates to a religious theme, story, legend, super hero comic book, song, or some other creative endeavor that can be relatable.

For example, during the 1960s and 1970s, many TV shows had "Computer Labs," such as the computer in the *Batman* TV series or the computers used in the *Six Million Dollar Man* series. On *Star Trek*, the crew of the USS Enterprise had hand-held communicators and computers as well. There are clips of these shows on YouTube.

The newspaper comic strip *Dick Tracy* featured a super detective who had a wristwatch that he used to communicate with his colleagues and could even see computer readouts. All of these fictional TV shows appeared decades before the personal computer, the smart phone, or even Apple's "Watch" were invented. Indeed, Apple's CEO Tim Cook even credits Dick Tracy and his wristwatch as being the inspiration for Apple's Watch.

All of these cultural references can be used in a paper on technology. The point here is to think and analyze: once you have researched your topic and have an understanding of it, make comparisons to things that you already know and with which you are familiar. It would be perfectly acceptable to begin a paper on "smart watches" (Apple's Watch) with a reference to Dick Tracy.

Some of the world's "newest" ideas are, in fact, not so "new." For example, although most historians would agree that the atom was not discovered until the 19th Century, the Greek philosopher Democritus established the theory of atomization around the year 400 BC—that's about 2300 years before moderns discovered the atom. Of course, Democritus's idea of atoms was a bit primitive, but his concept was close enough to how we understand atoms today.

In our case, we're going to use a few different sources and references to explain Telomeres, telomerase, the structure of both, and what leading scientists are saying about the potential of telomeres and telomerase and their impact on aging and cancer. Many genetic scientists believe that telomeres and its enzyme telomerase hold the answers to aging and cancer as these genetic pieces play a critical role in protecting our cells during mitosis (cell divivision).

An obvious historical reference to tie into these scientific advances and aging is Ponce de Leon, the Spanish explorer (and governor of Puerto Rico) who searched Florida for the fabled "Fountain of Youth." There are also the examples from the Bible, such as Noah living to be

950 (human longevity). How can we tie these cultural and religious references to a paper on DNA science?

Then there is the *Phineas and Ferb* song, "The Aglet Song." An apt analogy for the telomere and its relation to the chromosome is the aglet on a shoelace. An aglet is the plastic piece on the end of the shoelace that keeps the shoelace from fraying. How can we tie these cultural and religious references to a paper on DNA science?

The Components of the Expository Paper

The "expository paper" is just another way of saying, "a paper devoted to explaining a thing." There are many different types of expository papers, including papers written in the first person, but on the high school and college levels, the paper will be written formally and in the third person. This means the author needs to leave out first person references, such as, "I think," and so on.

The author also needs to avoid using slang, Internet abbreviations, and colloquialisms. The basic format of an expository paper is five paragraphs: the introduction, three paragraphs that "fill out the details," and the conclusion. To be sure, an expository paper can exceed five paragraphs.

The expository paper may be broken down as follows (please ignore the first person usage here, this is only to simplify):

1. I believe this (introduction paragraph)

2. Here are three reasons why I believe this (three paragraphs with details)

3. That's why I believe this (conclusion paragraph)

In a sense, an expository paper is written in a similar approach to the way most pop stars write their songs: just as the listener has a clear idea of the song's meaning by the first verse, it should be clear to the reader what the topic is in an expository paper at the start.

The Introduction Paragraph

The opening line of an expository paper ought to stir the interests of a reader: writing an analogy or a twist on a cliché are typical ways of writing a "**hook**." Some other variations of the **hook** are:

1. *The Cordial Commentator:* where an ironic or amusing statement, joke, anecdote, teaser, or an amusing story draws in the reader.

   For example: Although the tobacco plant is generally associated with smoking and causing cancer, its use in genetic research appears to demonstrate promising results in cancer treatments.

2. *The Factoid Barker:* this is the most straightforward "hook" where mention of some fact is brought to the reader's attention, a sort of "did you know?" type of sentence:

   For example: Most students are taught that the Nazi invasion of Poland on September 1, 1939 started the Second World War. Yet what is often left unsaid is that a few weeks later, on September 17, the Soviet Union also invaded Poland.

3. *The Dictionary Elucidator:* Where a word or idea that is linked to the paper's topic is defined.

   For example: To elucidate means to expound and explain; research attempting to illuminate the art of elucidation is abound.

4. *The Questioner:* This one directly raises a question and then answers it, although some teachers may warn against using a question to begin a research paper.

   For example: Are science and religion really at odds? In 1961, Dr. Leonard Hayflick discovered that human cells can only divide between 40 and 60 times before dying which, according to the math, maximizes a human lifespan at 120 years. A passage in the Book of Genesis, 6:3 claims that the maximum number of years for a human is 120 years.

There are a number of other types of **hooks**, but these four examples will suffice.

The follow-up sentence, often called the "**Topic Sentence,**" should explain the "five Ws" (who, what, where, when, and why) and, if possible, the "how." In fact, if you were to delete the "hook," the **topic sentence** could be used as the "lead" sentence; yet this is not to imply that the hook is superfluous. The **topic sentence** should be "overarching," meaning it should be general enough to tap into common knowledge while addressing a specific topic and giving the reader a clear idea of what he or she is about to read.

After the **Topic Sentence,** one to three sentences explaining the research and sources that were selected should be added. Think of this as a "**list,**" like a list people make before they go to the grocery store. These one-to-three sentences can be a quick summary of the research. Make sure you make at least three points that will later be given more detail in the three **body paragraphs**.

The final sentence of the introduction paragraph should be a strong, clear statement or argument, which is known as a "**thesis statement.**" This is no time to be wishy-washy: your **thesis statement** should be bold and forthright. This is where you strongly declare what you have discovered or, in the case of an argumentative paper, what you believe. The thesis sentence must be written definitively and with a "transition" in mind: the beginning of the second paragraph needs to relate to the introduction paragraph.

Body Paragraphs

Your three body paragraphs should each have a fact with evidence backing it up. Each one of these facts already appear in your **list** sentence that appears in your introduction paragraph. Your evidence should be a direct quote from an author or authority, or you paraphrasing something an author or authority on the subject claimed. The body paragraphs should also include critical or opposing views as well as views with which you agree.

Concluding Paragraph

Your concluding paragraph should consist of a summary of the paper and a "bang" at the end: a stronger statement than the thesis statement. Do NOT begin the concluding paragraph with "As you can see" or "In conclusion." Although both of these are acceptable in the context with some papers, both "transitions" break the rules of (1) avoiding the first person and (2) stating the obvious.

Solid research is the key to effective writing. If your research is sloppy and superficial, your research paper will be sloppy, superficial, and unfocused. If your research stinks, writing the opening paragraph to a paper will be a far more difficult task. As they say in computer programming: "garbage in, garbage out," also known by the acronym, "GIGO." If a line of code does not work or is input incorrectly, the result will also be incorrect.

Grammar and Stuff

Transitional Words and Phrases and Prepositional Phrases

Transitional words and phrases "smooth out" an essay or research paper. They help connect one idea to another and provide a way of tying previous ideas to new ideas. Think of transitional words and phrases like a person in the snow making tracks: each footprint is an idea helped along by the previous footsteps that logically brings us from the first to last footprint. Just as each footprint goes in a certain direction, transitional words and phrases connect each idea.

Many times a transitional word or phrase contains a preposition. A preposition is an enabler to a noun: the noun is going to do "something" and the preposition helps "bring" the noun to that action or thing. For example: I walk to the grocery store. In this example, "I" is the subject, "walk" is the verb, "grocery store" is the object of the preposition. The preposition is "to," which is helping me "walk" to the grocery store.

Another example: She jumped into the pool. "She" is the noun, "into" is enabling or giving the reader "direction" to where the noun (she) is jumping (verb).

To clarify, not all prepositions are transitions and not all transitions are prepositions. Transitions are about connecting ideas whereas prepositions are modifying a noun. To make a bad analogy, transitions are the "big picture," moving ideas whereas prepositions are "small picture," moving a subject to an object, for example.

You should never end sentence with a preposition or else you'll incur the wrath of the grammar police.

Another general rule in determining a preposition is if you remove that part of the sentence, the remaining part of the sentence will still make sense. To determine if a part of a sentence is a prepositional phrase, use the following formula:

The fly flew _____ the bottle.

Any word that fits into the "blank" and makes sense is a preposition and therefore, that part of the sentence is a prepositional phrase. Some words that fit in the "blank" are: in, above, along, inside, outside, around, below, past, at, by, under, beyond, and after. There are many other words that fit in the "blank." The only preposition that fits in the "blank" but does not sound "correct" is the word "of," which is a mighty preposition. There are other exceptions to the "Fly formula," but the purpose here is to give general rules (hopefully, your English and language arts teachers will go into further details on this subject and will not become catatonic should they read these general guidelines).

The following is a partial list of transitional words and phrases. Take note of the relationship between transitional words and phrases and prepositional phrases:

> ***Adding to an Idea:*** next, further, also, besides, in addition, moreover, furthermore, moreover, too, also, again, last, finally, furthermore, first, second, third (avoid using "firstly, secondly, thirdly, etc."). "Furthermore" is one of those "power additions."
>
> *Note:* "Addition" can also be used in the same sence as "Time and Sequence."
>
> ***Time and Sequence (like "Addition"):*** later on, first of all, to begin with, in the first place, at

the same time, for now, for the time being, the next step, in time, in turn, at first, next, then, soon, meantime, meanwhile, later, while, earlier, simultaneously, and afterward. "In conclusion" is acceptable, but do not use it.

"What Follows" or Consequence: accordingly, as a result, consequently, hence, otherwise, so then, therefore, thus, thereupon.

Compare and Contrast: These are stock for every "compare and contrast" assignment teachers give. Use them wisely: conversely, instead, by the same token, but, but by the same token, but as well, in contrast, likewise, on the one hand, on the other hand, rather, similarly, yet, but, still, nevertheless, on the contrary, yet, as of yet, nevertheless, nonetheless, after all, however, though, otherwise, to the contrary, notwithstanding, on the other hand, and at the same time.

The Over-view or Generalizing: as a rule, as usual, for the most part, conventional wisdom claims, generally, generally speaking, ordinarily, and usually. Avoid philosophical condurdums like, "who am I to say what is 'normal?'" Save that question for your philosophy class.

"To Repeat Myself without Looking Like I am Repeating Myself" or Restatement: in essence, in other words, namely, that is, in short, in brief, to put it differently, as previously stated, in a nutshell (this one could be flagged as a "colloquialism," which is informal), and that is to say.

Side Note or Diversion: by the way, incidentally, one other thing, one last thing (make sure it is the last thing you are addressing), and in a related topic or in a related fashion.

Analogy or Illustration: for example, for instance, for one thing, likewise, similar, moreover, and as further demonstrated or "demonstrably."

Direction and Time: while, now, opposite, beyond, never, after, later, earlier, always, when, soon, immediately, once, whenever, meanwhile, sometimes, in the mean time, during, afterwards, until, next, following, then, at length, simultaneously, so far, this time, subsequently, here, there, over there, nearly, under, above, to the left, to the right, and in the distance.

"This is the End" or Summarizing: after all, all in all, all things considered, briefly, by and large, in any case, in any event, in brief, on the whole, in short, in the final analysis, in the long run, on balance, in summary, on the whole, and finally. Never EVER end an essay or research paper with, "In conclusion."

Punctuation

Punctuation is what we call the marks that helps readers along with our writing: period, comma, parenthesis, quotation marks, colons, semicolons, and so on. You don't want to over-punctuate or under-punctuate.

The comma is the most controversial of the punctuation marks because nobody really knows for sure when and where to use it. Many people overdo the comma whearas some underuse the comma. So let's try to make the grammar police happy with a brief explanation of comma use.

1. Commas should be used after a longer, introductory type of clause in a sentence, such as, "We believe in the Freedom of Religion in the United States, except when it comes to human sacrifice." This is the correct use of a comma.

   An incorrect use would be, "We believe in the Freedom of Religion, in the United States, except when it comes to human sacrifice." In this instance, we have a short prepositional phrase and although it may appear "correct" to place a comma at the end of the first preposition, the comma only confuses the reader.

2. Do not use commas in a short prepositional phrase. For example, "During Halloween, kids get dressed up as goblins." Just leave the comma out: "During Halloween kids get dressed up as goblins." One other thing: while it may sound okay to use "dressed up as goblins" in this part of the sentence, the "up" is not necessary: a better phrase would be, "kids get dressed as goblins."

3. Use a commas to split independent clauses that are joined by conjunctions. If you've forgotten what an independent clause is, it's merely a fancy way of saying "simple sentence." It can stand on its own and still make sense. But as we venture into the world of compound sentences and use conjunctions, we must always use a comma before the conjunction. For example: "I like to go fishing and avoid going to school, and some

people call this truancy whereas I call it playing hooky."

A Few More Things about Punctuation

1. Always use the space bar after putting in a comma, period, semicolon (;), colon (:), somebody's initials (D.A. Johnson), after an abbreviation, question mark, exclamation point, and before and after an ampersand (&, if your teacher allows this).

2. In the days of typewriters and mechanical leading, it used to be standard to hit the spacebar twice after each sentence. Since most people are using computers and word processors like Microsoft Word, it is unnecessary to use a "double space bar" after each period, unless your teacher says otherwise.

3. Quotation marks are used to indicate a quote from a direct source. Also use quotation marks also around newspaper, magazine and Internet articles, chapters from a book, conferences and lectures, and reports. If the person giving a lecture does not tell you the title of the lecture, create an appropriate name for it (i.e., "Lecture on Mitosis"). Song titles are in quotation marks, CDs or Album titles are italicized.

Italics

Use italics to indicate a magazine, novel, play, newspaper or online organization. Italics are also used for published works, movies, and album names (music).

Some Grammar Rules

Once again, we can't cover every grammatical rule here, but we can touch on the important and most used grammar rules.

1. Singular verbs and pronouns go with singular subjects. Some pronouns are always singular; do not use them with plural subjects. Ever. Pronouns that are always singular are: anybody, everybody, everyone, no one (NEVER spell it "noone"), nobody, one, each, either, and neither.

2. Some singular pronouns may be singular or plural, depending on the noun. This is really one of the annoying parts about grammar, but there it is: exceptions to the rule. Such singular pronouns that may be either singular or plural (depending on the noun) are: all, any, more, most, none, and some. Sigh…

3. Use plural verbs and plural pronouns with plural subjects. Do this always.

And that's enough.

Notes

_____

_____

_____

_____

_____

_____

_____

_____

_____

_____

_____

_____

11 Setting up Stylesheets in MS Word

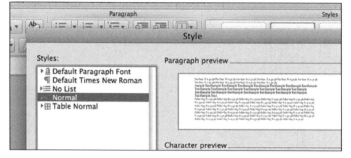

Figure 11.1: The Style palette on the Mac.

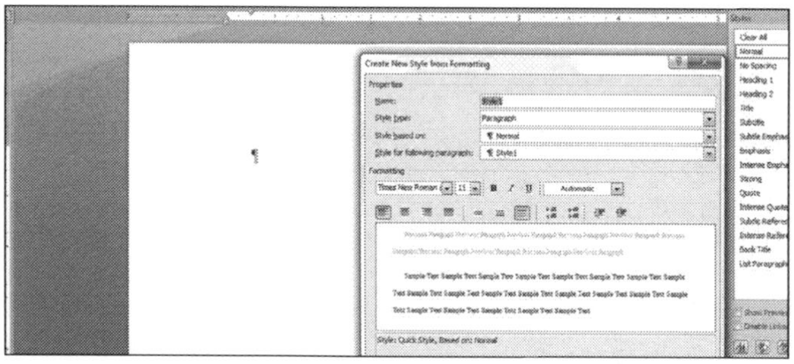

Figure 11.2: The Style palette in Windows.

NOW THAT YOU ARE FAMILIAR and somewhat of an expert with the Paragraph formatting palette, let's go to Stylesheets, how to set them up, and save them so you don't keep repeating the same steps. To be sure, computers were initially invented to take care of repetitious tasks such as formatting a research paper. The good thing about Stylesheets is that once they are set and saved, you can use them as long as you have the program loaded onto your computer.

Before we get started, let's define "stylesheet": it's a sort of template that is built into a computer program were "styles" can be designed and used in multiple and subsequent projects. A stylesheet basically contains layouts, fonts, linespacing, and other "styles" used in printing and on the World Wide Web. When a stylesheet is applied, all the elements in a document (fonts, font sizes, indentations, even graphics) are set to the user's specifications.

So, in the case of an MLA formatted paper, there would be two style sheets created: (1) MLA Text and (2) MLA Works Cited. There are other various parts, such as a "block quote," that can also be added to stylesheets, but let's keep it simple for now.

Since MS Word on the Mac is slightly more "complicated," the steps written here will be for the Mac; however, both the Mac and Windows environment will be demonstrated here with screenshots.

The Task

Open the file you created to write the expository paper on telomeres and telomerase (page 33, "MLA Formatting: The Expository Research Paper"). Take your cursor and highlight the first paragraph. On the Mac, go into Format>>Style (**Figure 11.3**), in Windows, click on the Styles bar in the Home Ribbon (**Figure 11.4**).

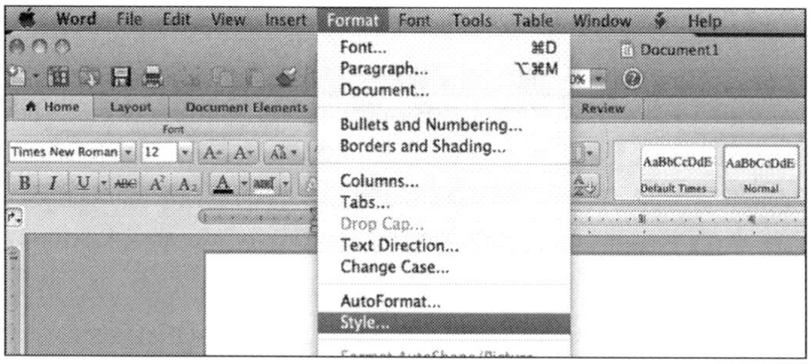

Figure 11.3: Getting to the Stylesheet on the Mac.

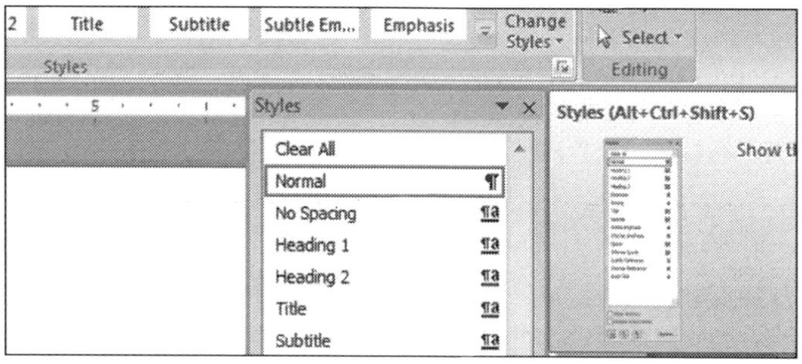

Figure 11.4: Getting to the Stylesheet in Windows.

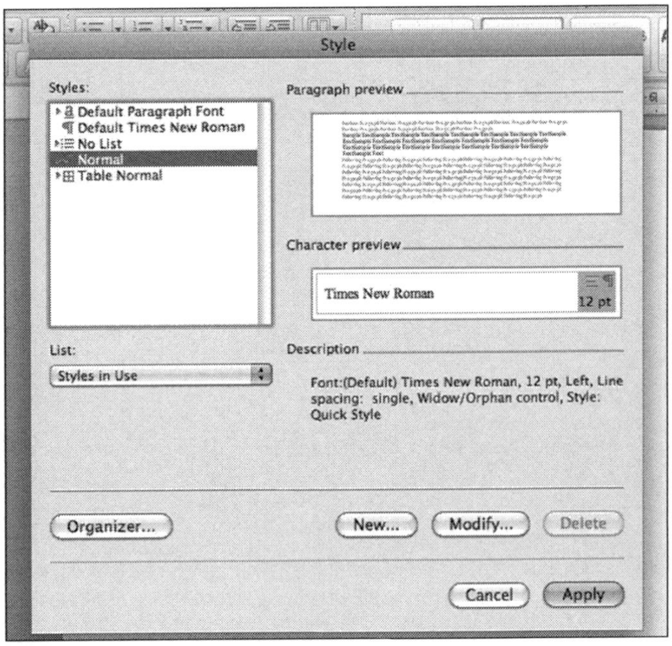

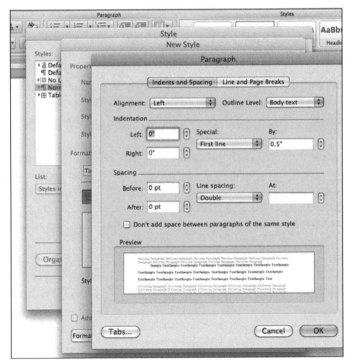

Figure 11.5: By clicking on the "New..." button, a new palette will appear so a new Stylesheet can be created with new paragraph properties (font, line spacing, etc.). The Style palette is very similar in the Windows platform.

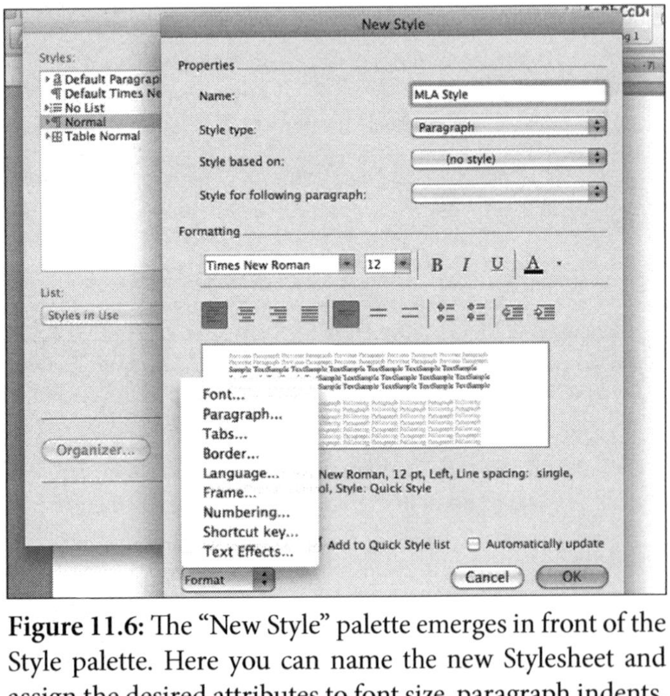

Figure 11.6: The "New Style" palette emerges in front of the Style palette. Here you can name the new Stylesheet and assign the desired attributes to font size, paragraph indents, and line spacing. Line-spacing and indents can be accessed by accessing the "Format" button on the lower-left corner of the palette box. For MLA formatting, you are really only going to use the main area of the New Style palette and the "Paragraph" selection in the "Format" button, which will bring up yet another dialog box. Once all your settings are correct, select the "OK" button and you'll return to the Style palette. Again, the set up is similar in Windows.

On the lower part of the Style palette, select the "New" button, which will launch the New Style palette. Name the new style "MLA Text." Make sure the Style type is set to "Paragraph." The "Style based on" area should read "no style." Ignore the area that reads, "Style for following paragraph." (see **Figures 11.5** and **11.6**).

In the New Style palette, you can set the font (Times New Roman, 12 Point). By clicking on the "Format" button (**Figure 11.6**, again), you can set the parameters for a paragraph by selecting "Paragraph" (**Figure 11.7**). Does this palette look familiar? Make sure the appropriate values are put in correctly: Double spaced and that the indents are set under "Special," First Line and 0.5". If you used the tab key to indent, you will have to go back and delete these (make sure your invisible or "non-printing characters" are turned on).

Also, make sure the "After" setting in the Paragraph palette's Spacing area is set to "0 pt."

When you are finished, select "OK." This will bring you back to the New Style palette. Along the bottom of

Figure 11.7: Most of the formatting for the MLA style takes place in this palette. Access it through the Style>>New Style palettes, those settings (font style, size, line-spacing, etc.) can be saved and used as a template for future MLA-style papers. For paragraphs, you want to make sure the Indentation is set to First line by 0.5" and make sure that the Line spacing is double. When you set your Indents to First line by 0.5", make sure that whatever tabs you used to manually indent your paragraphs are deleted (which can be seen by having "non-printing" characters turned on).

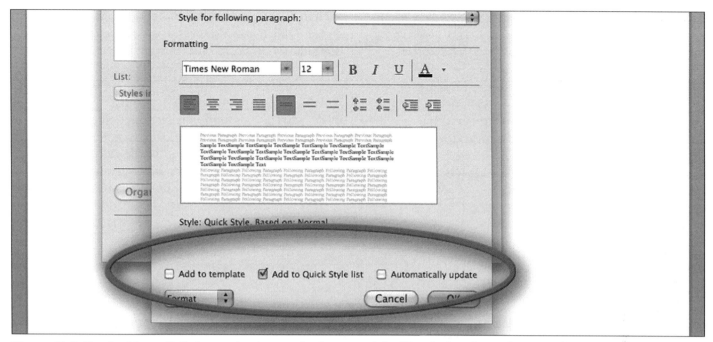

Figure 11.8: By checking off all three selections at the bottom of the New Style palette, the MLA format is saved and ready for the next time you have to write an MLA-style paper.

the palette are checkboxes for Add to template, Add to Quick Style list, and Automatically update. Click all three checkboxes (**Figure 11.8**).

Double-check to see if you named the new style (MLA Text). Now click the "OK" button on the lower right corner of the New Style palette. Now the Style palette will be prominent. Select the "Apply" button on the lower right corner of the Style palette.

Congratulations: you just created a stylesheet. It should appear in the Quick Style list in your toolbar (both Mac and Windows).

Now create a stylesheet for the Works Cited entries. Follow the same steps and name it "MLA Works Cited." This time, when you get to the Paragraph palette, select "Hanging" under the Special area in the Indentation section (**Figure 11.9**) and be sure it reads: By 0.5".

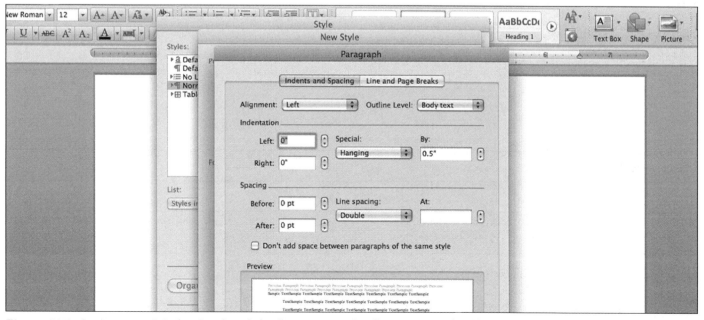

Figure 11.9: Setting up a Works Cited and the "Hanging Indent" in MS Word. All the characteristics are Left alignment, Hanging indent By 0.5", and double line-spacing.

Grammar and Organization of Works Cited Entries

We're going to focus on six of the most frequently used entries for a Works Cited page: (1) the Internet, (2) printed book, (3) printed magazine or newspaper article (4) class lecture, (5) image or graphic and (6) image or graphic where the author is unknown. There are many other sources and the Internet is loaded with examples. If you use a source and get stumped, go to a search engine such as Google or Yahoo! and input "MLA Citation for _____" and input whatever it is you were using (video, YouTube video, etc.).

Remember, not every Web site gives a date the article was posted or an author name. Also, all "Works Cited" entries are in alphabetical order. This is very tedious work and nobody really likes doing it so keep in mind that messing up a Works Cited page may not only leave you open for accusations of plagiarism, but perhaps "points off," as every teacher has attended college and had to write papers with Works Cited and so on.

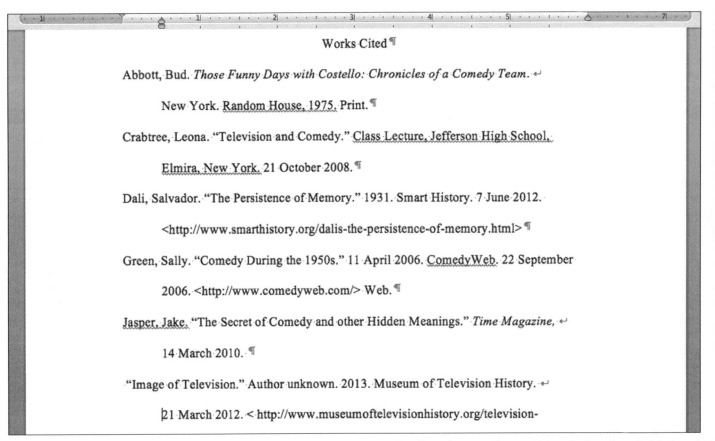

Works Cited

Abbott, Bud. *Those Funny Days with Costello: Chronicles of a Comedy Team.*

New York. Random House, 1975. Print.

Crabtree, Leona. "Television and Comedy." Class Lecture, Jefferson High School,

Elmira, New York. 21 October 2008.

Dali, Salvador. "The Persistence of Memory." 1931. Smart History. 7 June 2012.

<http://www.smarthistory.org/dalis-the-persistence-of-memory.html>

Green, Sally. "Comedy During the 1950s." 11 April 2006. ComedyWeb. 22 September

2006. <http://www.comedyweb.com/> Web.

Jasper, Jake. "The Secret of Comedy and other Hidden Meanings." *Time Magazine,*

14 March 2010.

"Image of Television." Author unknown. 2013. Museum of Television History.

21 March 2012. <http://www.museumoftelevisionhistory.org/television-

Figure 11.10: This is how a Works Cited page should look. Notice that "Works Cited" is NOT underlined or bolded and is centered. Also take note that there is no extra linespacing between each entry. Reminder: A Works Cited page is always started within a document; you should use "Insert>>Page break to begin the fresh page. If the last page in your paper was page 4, then the Works Cited should begin on page 5.

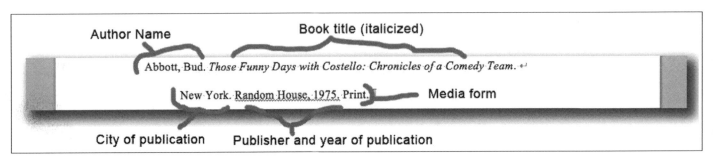

Figure 11.11: Book entry. Book, movie, and periodical titles are always italicized.

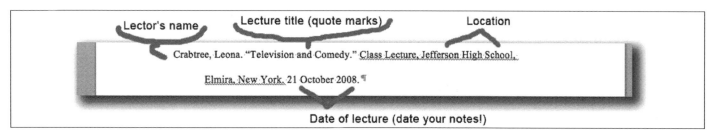

Figure 11.12: Lecture or Speaker's Entry. As long as you're taking notes in class and you date them, you can use classroom lectures and what your teachers say during class. This is also the correct form for guest speakers who address schools and other institutions. You're already doing the work by taking notes, so use that information. Don't worry about being called an "apple polisher."

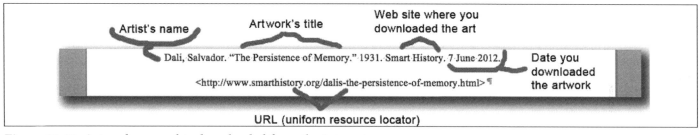

Figure 11.13: Artwork or graphic downloaded from the Internet.

Figure 11.14: Artwork or graphic downloaded from the Internet with no author name or author credit.

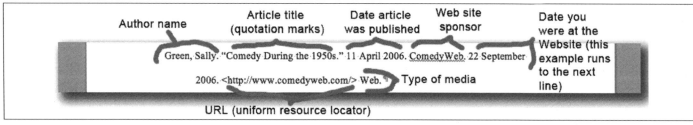
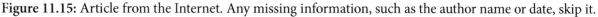

Figure 11.15: Article from the Internet. Any missing information, such as the author name or date, skip it.

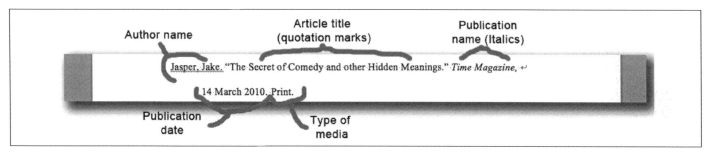

Figure 11.16: Article from a magazine, newspaper, or printed periodical.

12 Working in Columns, Setting Leader Lines, and Using Word Art

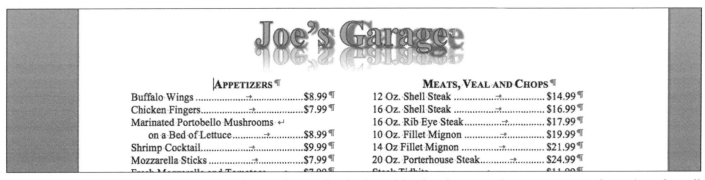

Figure 12.1: A mockup menu using WordArt, columns, leader lines (the dots between the menu item and price), and small caps. All of these features will be covered in this section.

Mᴉᴄʀᴏsᴏғᴛ Wᴏʀᴅ can be used for laying out newsletters and other visually-oriented objects such as menus, party invitations, awards lists, concert participation rosters, and even visual or illustrated stories. Columns are one way of "squeezing" more text onto a page in a visually appealing way.

The Restaurant Menu: The Task

You're a chef at a restaurant. It's time to change the dinner menu. You'll need the following:

- Menu items for appetizers, salads, soups, fish, chicken, desserts, etc. (See Example).

- The menu item section "headers" have to "pop," so they need to be in boldface type and small caps (e.g., Sᴛᴇᴀᴋs ᴀɴᴅ Cʜᴏᴘs, Sᴀʟᴀᴅs, etc.). Keep these sections in 13 point, Times New Roman Bold Font.

- Also, include prices. This means you will need what's called a "leader line," sometimes "dots" or other characters that help readers match items from one side of the page to the other. For example:

Lambchops..$18.95

- Font size for menu items should be 11 pt., Times New Roman

- Using "Word Art," create a restaurant name that will appear centered at the top of the page.

Launch Microsoft Word, create a new file, and save it appropriately.

1. Make sure the "Ruler" at the top of the page is turned on (Mac: View menu>>Rulers; Windows: View tab, check "Ruler").

2. Setting columns: In Windows, click on the Page Layout tab and select the icon indicating two columns. On the Mac, go to the Format menu, select "Columns," and select "two." The column widths will default to 3". This measurement is important, as you will have to use this measurement for setting your tabs and "leader lines."

3. Begin inputting your menu item section headers and menu items and prices: don't worry about formatting for now. Make sure to hit the tab key only once in between the menu items

APPETIZERS

Buffalo Wings $8.99
Chicken Fingers $7.99
Marinated Portobello Mushrooms
    on a Bed of Lettuce $8.99
Shrimp Cocktail $9.99
Mozzarella Sticks...$7.99
Fresh Mozzarella and Tomatoes $7.99
Potato Skins $6.99
Nachos...$6.99
Fried Clams and Tartar Sauce $7.99

SALADS

Garden Salad..$4.99
Caesar Salad...$5.99
Spinach Salad...$5.99
Ham and Provolone Salad................................$7.99
Oyster and Herring Salad.................................$9.99
Fruit Salad..$8.99
Lobster Salad $12.99
Healthy Green Salad $3.99

DESSERT

Chocolate Mousse..$7.99
Ice Cream (Check for
    Available Flavors)......................................$7.99
Pie (Banana, Blueberry, Apple
    and Cherry) $8.99
Chocolate Forrest Cake....................................$7.99
Coconut Souffle with
    Chocolate Sauce...$8.99
Chocolate Souffle $9.99

PASTA

Penne alla Vodka...$11.99
Shrimp Provencal..$16.99
Fettuccini Alfredo with Chicken
    and Sweet Italian Sausage.......................$14.99
Chicken and Portobello Mushrooms
    over Spiral Pasta $12.99
Veal Scallopini in Pesto over Bow
    Tie Pasta...$14.99

STEAKS, VEAL, AND CHOPS

12 Oz. Shell Steak..$14.99
16 Oz. Shell Steak..$16.99
16 Oz. Rib Eye Steak $17.99
8 Oz. Fillet Mignon...$19.99
12 Oz Fillet Mignon..$22.99
20 Oz. Porterhouse Steak $24.99
Steak Tidbits...$11.99
Veal Cutlet Parmigiana $14.99
Veal Rollatini $14.99
Veal Marsala..$14.99

CHICKEN

Bar-B-Q Chicken Quarters................................$13.99
Chicken Marsala $12.99
Chicken Scallopini with
    Mushrooms and Onions $12.99
Chicken Francese $12.99
Chicken Cutlet Parmigiana $12.99
Chicken Kiev $12.99
Chicken Scarpariello...$12.99
Grilled Chicken and Mushrooms.....................$12.99
Garlic Sauteed Chicken and
    Mushrooms $12.99
Chicken and Hot Italian Sausage
with Lemon-Garlic Sauce $12.99
Sesame Chicken with Squash and
    Carrots in Rutabaga Sauce......................$14.99

FISH AND SEAFOOD

Shrimp Scampi...$16.99
Crusted Shrimp in Garlic Sauce.....................$16.99
Shrimp Kabob..$16.99
Shrimp Primavera $16.99
Sauteed Shrimp, Scallops, and
    Lobster Tails in Beurre
    Blanc Sauce..$24.99
Broiled Bluefish $12.99
Grilled Tuna in Lemon Caper
    Sauce...$18.99
Grilled Mako Shark with
    Mushrooms and Onions $16.99

and prices. The leader lines will be set up in the Tabs section in the Paragraph palette later. For menu items, use the sample menu on the opposite page. When you are finished inputting the information, organize and format the menu.

4. Highlight all the text by selecting Edit>>Select all or the shortcut keys (Mac, Command + A or Windows, Control + A). Go into the Paragraph Formatting palette. The names of some menu items may take up more than one line, so set the "Hanging Indent" by .25". Select the OK button.

   Go into the Tabs section (through the Paragraph Formatting Palette). Input 2.25" in the "Tab stop position." This number was selected so there will be enough room to fit the prices (remember, the column size defaults to 3", so it makes sense to leave a little room after the leader line (see **Figure 12.2**).

   Make sure your Default tab stops is set at .25". Leave the alignment set to Left. In the "Leader" section, click on the button that indicates .... (it some versions of MS Word, it may look like 2................). Now Select "OK."

5. The "Soft Return" or "Soft Enter." A "Soft Return" is different than a "Hard Return" in Microsoft Word in a number of ways. Primarily, a "Soft Return" is used to keep the formatting of a line of text, whereas a "Hard Return" will always start a new paragraph. For example, the third menu item in the example menu provided

| Appetizers |
| Buffalo Wings.........................$9.46 |
| Chicken Fingers ....$7.99 |
| Marinated Portobello Mushrooms on a Bed of Lettuce ....$8.99 |
| Shrimp Cocktail ....$9.99 |

Figure 12.3: Text flowing "incorrectly" and running out of sync with the other menu items.

| Appetizers ¶ |
| Buffalo·Wings........................→...............$12.46 ¶ |
| Chicken·Fingers ....→.........$7.99 ¶ |
| Marinated·Portobello·Mushrooms ↵ |
| on·a·Bed·of·Lettuce.........→.........$8.99 ¶ |
| Shrimp·Cocktail ¶ |

Figure 12.4: By using a "soft return" ("soft enter"), which is holding down the shift key while striking the return or enter key, you can maintain the characteristics of the paragraph.

takes up two lines in the column and doesn't "look right" (**Figure 12.3**).

By striking the Enter/Return key ("Hard Return"), a new line will appear, which will then cause the "hanging indent" to disappear. The correct way is to use a "Soft Return." Place the cursor in the area where the sentence will "look good," hold down the shift key and press "Return/Enter." If nonprinting characters are turned on, instead of ¶, the nonprinting paragraph marker, a bent arrow pointing to the left will appear. By using the "Soft Return," the hanging indent will remain and the text flow will "look right" (see **Figure 12.4**). Make sure to fix other menu items that take up more than one line.

6. Menu Item Section Headers should be bold, and in small caps (see **Figure 12.5**). The Menu Item Sections are: Appetizers; Salads; Dessert; Pasta; Meats, Veal, and Chops; Chicken; Fish and Seafood. Make sure these headers are 13 point and in the Times New Roman bold font. Again, make sure the menu items are 11 point and in the Times New Roman font.

7. Once you align the Appetizers, Salads, Dessert, and Pasta items in the left column, go to Insert>>Column Break (Mac). In Windows, go to the Page Layout tab and insert column break.

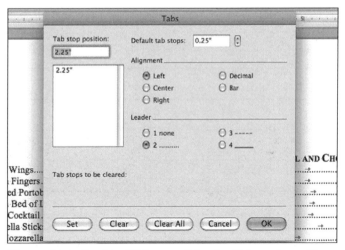

Figure 12.2: Setting "Tab stops" in the Tabs palette. Since the default size for columns in MS Word is 3" a column, be sure to input 2.25".

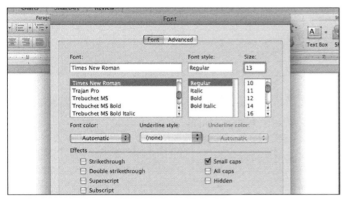

Figure 12.5: The Fonts palette (Format>>Fonts on the Mac; Home>>Font in Windows). Special design characteristics can be set in this palette. It is also accessible through the Stylesheets palette under Style>>New Style>>Format (see pages 41—43).

This will ensure that there is no text "backflow" and will keep these items in the left column (rather than you constantly trying to make it fit by using the Enter/Return key or the backspace/delete key). Now "fit" the remaining text into the right column (Steaks, Chicken, Fish, etc.).

8. Place your cursor to the top of the page. Go to Insert>>WordArt. You will see placeholder text that reads, "Your Text Here." Type in the name you've given your restaurant. Feel free to play around with the various effects and modes available. Make sure that the length of the box for the WordArt reaches the 6.5" wide on the ruler at the top of the document (see **Figure 12.6**).

   If there is text from the menu items "hidden" behind the WordArt, click on the right of the box and extend the length.

   If the WordArt needs to be moved because it is not placed at the top, click and drag it to its proper position.

If for some reason your WordArt is hidden behind the text, select the WordArt and then right-click (Windows) or Control + Click (Mac). Select the "Wrap Text" option from the pop-up menu. Usually the "Square" option will set the WordArt right.

Feel free to fool around with fonts and change them. Just keep the point sizes the same. Take note that some fonts at 12-point may appear "larger" than others at the 12-point size. This has more to do with the shape of the font.

9. On the Mac, select the WordArt file and then "Control + Click"; on the PC, right-click on the mouse (after the WordArt has been selected). A popup menu will appear (see **Figures 12.7** and **12.8**). Choose "Format Text Effect." Play around with the effect selections on the left side of the palette. You can always delete it and redo if it gets too messy.

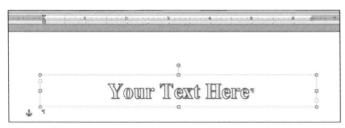

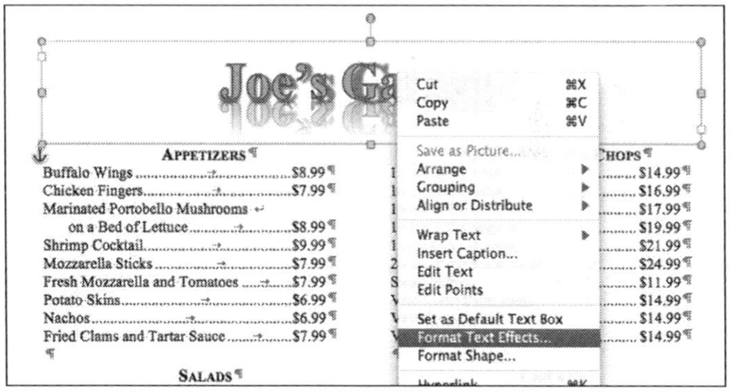

Figure 12.7: By right-clicking (Windows) or Control + clicking (Mac), a popup menu offering a number of style options appears. Selecting "Format Text Effects" brings the user to "cool" effects, such as mirroring, colorizing, and so on.

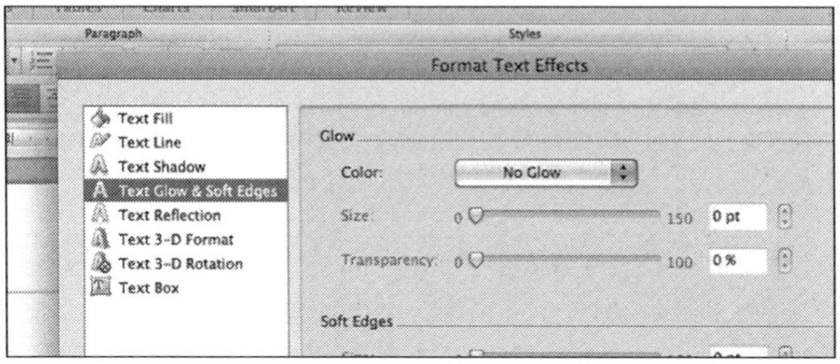

Figure 12.6: Placeholder text for WordArt. In this case, click on one of the corner points and stretch it so it is at least 6.5" inches wide.

Figure 12.8: Take some time to play around with the effects.

13 Working with Tables I: The Sixteen Panel Illustrated Story

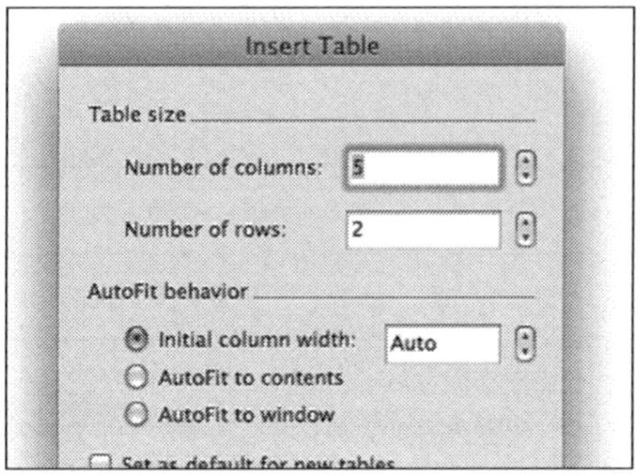

Figure 13.1: By going to the Table menu and selecting Insert>>Table, the user can set the number of columns and rows necessary for a table. Columns and rows can be added or deleted, resized and even "split."

Using the table feature in Microsoft Word, create a 16 panel illustrated story. The story can be anything: children's story, cartoon, something related to a holiday, or something not serious. Or something serious. Whatever you wish.

Each panel will have an image, so you will need 16 images. Images can be created using Photoshop or Paint (if you're not artistic, stick figures will work). Or you can use clip art (Insert>>ClipArt). There are a numerous Websites that offer free clip art.

If you want to use Photo Booth (the program is available for both Macs and PCs), that is another option open to you. But tell a story: make sure it follows a logical sequence. Make sure the progression of the story reads from left to right.

Go into your class folder and create a new folder. Make sure your view option for the folders is in the List mode, not "Icons" or "Small Icons." Name it in the correct numerical sequence and place an underscore and "PanelStory" at the end (i.e., 12Jones_PanelStory).

Inside that folder, create another folder, name it "PanelStory_Images." This is where you are going to save the images that will be used in your story. As you create or gather images, be sure to save them to this folder.

Close out of the folders, launch Microsoft Word, save the file in the first folder (i.e., 12Jones_PanelStory). Give the file the same name as the folder in which it is saved.

The Task

1. Set the page orientation to "Landscape." This is basically turning the page "sideways." Go to the Layout tab, look for "Orientation." Select "Landscape" (the default is "Portrait").

2. Click on the Tables tab and hover the mouse on the "New" table icon (see **Figure 13.2**; it looks a little like a tic tac toe setup). You'll see a series of empty boxes (called "cells") in the hover menu. As you mouse over the boxes, the palette will indicate the number of cells your hovering represents. This is a nice feature, but go to the bottom of the palette and select "Insert Table."

3. A dialogue box will appear. Since this is going to be a 16-panel, illustrated story, input 4 in both the "Number of columns" and "Number of rows" dialogue fields. Make sure the "Autofit behavior" is set to "Initial column width," and the selection reads "Auto." This is the default setting in Word.

4. In the first cell, type anything—gibberish or a full sentence. When you type gibberish, make sure you hit the space bar every five or six characters. Fill the cell with enough text so that it is

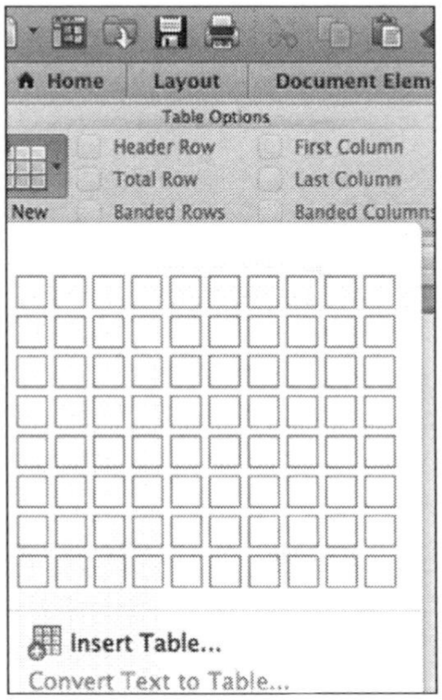

Figure 13.2: The Table tool in the Tables Ribbon offers a visual way to select the number of columns and rows (cells) in a table.

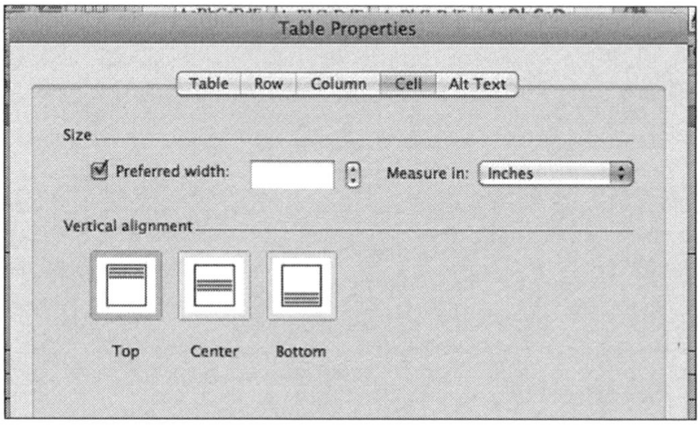

Figure 13.4: The Table Properties palette. In this area, you can set text, cell color, alignment, etc. This screen shot is here to indicate what the Table Properties palette looks like.

at least 4 lines long. Take note of how the cell expands southward (downwards) in the column and not "east-to-west." Columns maintain their widths but the "height" will expand. Delete the gibberish text.

5. By mousing over to the upper-left corner of the table, a "tool" (a box with a type of cross appears). This is called the "Table Control" (see **Figure 13.3**). Right-click (on the Mac, Control + Click) and a submenu appears with a list of functions. Select Table Properties (at the bottom of the list; see **Figure 13.4**).

This is a shortcut to a number of the same features found in the "ribbons" or tools. Different line styles can be applied to the table, as well as different colors to the table's background, as well as customizing borders to the page and so on.

Along the ribbon are a number of other options, including a pencil icon that if selected, will change the individual lines of cells within a table. So, if there was a cell that you wanted to highlight or emphasize, this would be the tool to use.

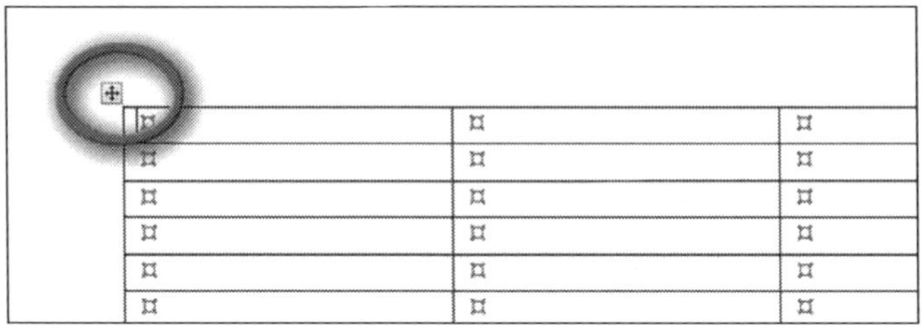

There are numerous other effects and objects that can be placed into individual cells, including charts from Microsoft Excel and other graphics.

Images can also be inserted into individual cells along with text. If the images are inserted first, then the text will appear below the image in a cell. If the text is typed first, then the image will appear below the text.

To resize an image (see **Figure 13.5**), click on the image and drag the corner points in (to shorten it) or out (to enlarge it, but this will also make the image appear "fuzzy"). Always resize an image by the corners so the image will maintain its proportions; if you select one of the middle selection points and drag, you will "warp" or distort the image.

The text and image layout can be adjusted by clicking on the image; once the image is selected, Format Picture

Figure 13.5: An image with text inside a table cell. By clicking on the image, points appear around the edges so the user can manipulate the image (resize, rotate, position, etc.).

Figure 13.3: The "Table Control".

will appear. There are a number of image filters and other photo accessories available, but the most commonly sought out features are Border (do you want to "draw" a

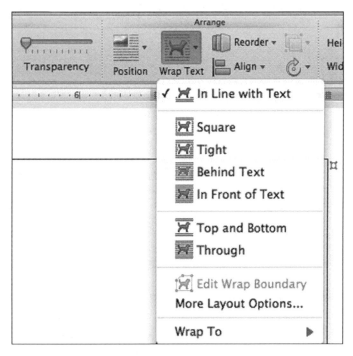

Figure 13.6: Wrapping text around an image. If your image is blocking text or making the text flow in an odd way, click on the image and the Format Picture tab will appear. Look for the "Wrap Text" icon. You can align the text and it relationship with the image by selecting the various choices (Square, Behind Text, In Front of Text, etc.). For Windows users, if the Wrap Text icon does not appear in your ribbon, double-click on the WordArt and it will appear in your ribbon.

border around the image?); Transparency (give the image a "faded" effect); Position (which arranges the image and text in a number of different "looks"); and Wrap Text (which is a big help when text is hidden behind an image; see **Figure 13.6**).

When an image is clicked-on, a bluish dot appears in the center-top; this is for rotating the image, which can be accomplished by mousing over the image and clicking and dragging in the direction desired.

The size of the cells can also be adjusted. By moving the mouse cursor over the lines, the cursor indicator will turn into an object with two arrows going in separate directions. Clicking and dragging can adjust the line.

When you are ready to place images in the panels, click on the individual panel where you want the image to appear, go to "Insert>>Photo>>Picture from file. Navigate to the "PanelStory_Images" folder.

This project will likely run two pages so include a running head with your last name followed by the page number. Depending on how the text flows and the size of the images, the bottom part of page one or the top part of page two may appear disjointed or look incorrect. This will happen mainly because of the screen and how the art and text is being "redrawn" on the monitor. If it looks "screwy," go into "print preview," which will give you a better indication how the file "really" looks.

> *Note:* Finally, if you get to the point where half of one row appears at the bottom of one page and the other half appears at the top of the next page, use "Insert>>Page Break." Go to the first cell of the bottom of the first page and insert Page Break. This will ensure that the table row begins on a new page.

Notes

_____

_____

_____

_____

_____

_____

_____

_____

_____

_____

14 Working with Tables II: Women Nobel Laureates and the Academic Table

Jones 1

Lisa Jones
Mr. Cornwalis
Science
14 October 2012

Women Nobel Laureates

Name	Date of Birth or Death	Year Received the Nobel Prize	Area of Science	Why the Nobel Prize was Awarded	

THE NOBEL PRIZE was established by the will of Alfred Nobel in 1895. Nobel was a Swedish inventor who is best known for the invention of dynamite. The first Nobel Prizes were given in the scientific categories of Chemistry, Physics, Medicine and Physiology, Literature and Peace. The award has been given each year since 1901. The Nobel Prize for Economics was established in 1969.

The Nobel Prizes come with a gold medallion, an honorary degree and around $1 million for each award. Many times the award has been given to multiple scientists who have worked together or separately on a discovery and have shared the prize.

Although there is a trend in education to promote science to girls as if women were never involved in science and it's a "man's field," this is untrue: good science only needs "proof," which has little to do with gender, race, and religion and everything to do with empirical evidence. However, men have dominated the field of science not because they are "smarter" than women, but because they have had more opportunities than women.

The fact is that women have been among Nobel Prize winners in the sciences from nearly the beginning of the prize. For example, Marie Curie shared the 1903 prize in Physics with her husband Pierre Curie and Henri Becquerel. Women's contribution to science has been acknowledged in the scientific community for over a century yet women are still underrepresented proportionately in the field today.

The reasons for why women are underrepresented in science remain controversial. Some academics and pundits blame sexism, whereas others explain that women make career choices based on their ability to balance family and a career.

Yet the history of women winning Nobel Prizes for their contributions to science does give us an insight into the progress of science and its contributions to humanity. Scientists are prone to stating, "I stand on the shoulders of giants," meaning that a current generation's scientific and academic progress rests on the "shoulders" (discoveries, theories, etc.) of previous generations.

By covering the women who won the Nobel Prize for science, we can get a rough-yet-incomplete trajectory of advancements in science, techniques, and understanding.

The majority of women on the list of women scientists worked cooperatively with men, some of whom were their husbands. Most of them did work under conditions that may be described by some as sexist; the fact that these women prospered is not only a testimony to these individual women, but also to the men who worked with them. For the women who partnered with men, science provides us a clear example of women and men working together for the betterment of humanity.

There's an old cliché that goes, "No man is an island," which is sometimes used to explain how humanity is interdependent. Most scientists work collaboratively. Many of these celebrated women were also mothers who raised children while excelling in science. To be sure, there are many heroic women today who who perhaps deserve their own international prize for their sacrifices as they work anonymously while raising children and taking care of other family members.

The Task

This project is going to be landscaped and in the MLA format except for line spacing, which will be single-spaced. Go into your class folder, be sure it is in the "list" view mode, create a new folder and correctly name it in the proper numerical sequence. Close out of the folder and launch Microsoft Word.

Create two Microsoft Word files: the first file will be saved with the same name as the folder followed by an underscore (_) and WomenScience (i.e., 13Jones_WomenScience). The second file will be named similarly with a different tag that reads "_WomenSciNotes" (i.e., 13Jones_WomenSciNotes). The second file will be used to input notes and keep track of sources.

Students will work in small groups or pairs and be assigned one or two of the following women who won a Nobel Prize for accomplishments in science:

Maria Goeppert-Mayer
Marie Curie
Irène Joliot-Curie
Dorothy Crowfoot Hodgkin
Gerty Theresa Cori
Rosalyn Yalow
Barbara Mcclintock
Rita Levi-Montalcini
Gertrude B. Elion
Christiane Nüsslein-Volhard
Linda B. Buck
Ada E. Yonath

Françoise Barré-Sinoussi
Elizabeth H. Blackburn
Carol W. Greider

Finally, identify Rosalind Franklin. Should she be on this list? Why isn't she included? Does she deserve an "Honorable Mention?"

Details

The name of the table should be:

Women Nobel Laureates

The category columns are as follows:

(1) Name (2) Date of Birth (and death if applicable) (3) Year Received Nobel Prize (4) Area of science prize was awarded (5) what the Nobel Prize was for (see **Figure 14.1**). The description of what the Nobel Prize was awarded for should be three to six sentences and in your own words. Do your best to understand and describe why the women were given the award. Make sure you cite your sources.

The category names should be in boldface, Times New Roman 12 point type. The information should be in Times New Roman, 12-point type. Use common sense when adjusting the column widths. For example, the description of what the Nobel Prize was for should be the widest column.

The most efficient way to move across a table and go from cell to cell is to use the tab key.

Columns and rows can be added by clicking on the column or row where you want the next column or row to appear and using Insert>> Columns to the Left, Columns to the Right or Rows Above or Rows Below. Columns and Rows can be deleted as well. Using a right-clicking (Windows) or Control + Click (Mac), this will bring up a menu offering some of these features as well.

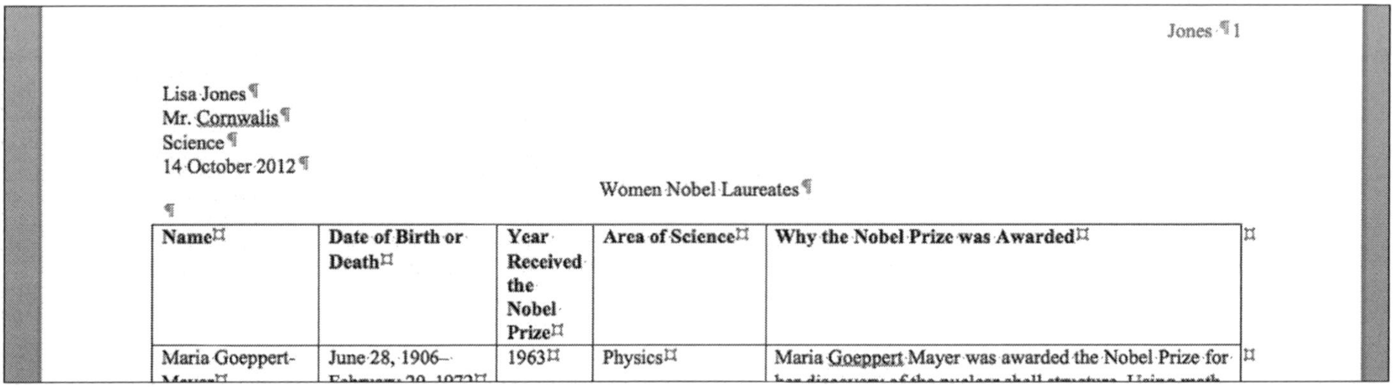

Figure 14.1: Landscaped layout example.

This table will be from 7 to 10 pages in length. Should a "widow" appear on a page (that's when one line or a word appears at the bottom of the page and the rest of the text appears on another page), use Insert>>Page Break to keep the information together on the next page. In other words, don't use the Enter/Return key to lengthen space; hitting the Enter/Return key in a cell will only enlarge the cell.

Students will work in groups from 2 to 4, each group will have two or three scientists, depending on the class size. They will use the Internet to find the necessary information and keep track of the Web sites visited.

Students will then report their research to the class regarding the scientist's birthday and date of death (if applicable), the year she won the award, the area of science and the three-to-five sentences describing why the scientist won. The entire class will input the information into their tables as each group reports its findings.

Although many of these scientists led fascinating lives, their biographical information is not a reason "why" they were awarded the Nobel Prize. Avoid getting tangled in the details: your job here is to explain in the simplest terms why a scientist was awarded with the prestigious Nobel Prize for science and "pare down" complex concepts in science.

Table Footnote: Also, in your own words, you are to write a paragraph below the table explaining what the Nobel Prize is, who Alfred Nobel was, and how scientists receive the award. The table footnote is to be done individually: the information in the table for the class will be uniform but the footnote is the individual part to this project (see **Figure 14.2**).

Be thorough in your explanation of Alfred Nobel how scientists receive the Nobel Prize: who nominates scientists? What is the process? How are scientists se-lected for the award? What is the award, is it money, a trophy, a fancy ceremony? If there's a ceremony, where is it held? Who is Alfred Nobel? What are some of his inventions? Why did he start the Nobel Prize? Are there any urban legends regarding the Nobel Prize?

The footnote should appear below the table: click outside the table to input text below the table. The non-printable characters should be turned on for this project.

The Nobel Prize Foundation's Website should be used as your primary source:

http://www.nobelprize.org/nobel_prizes/lists/women.html

You may use other Web sites as well. Keep track of your sources. You will be assessed on the readability of your table as well as the accuracy of your material. You are not to cut and paste information from the Web site when describing why these female scientists were given their award; again, please explain in your own words.

Make sure to include a Works Cited Page at the end of this. Some entries may not appear "normal" because they may take up only one line. Make sure the Works Cited page is also landscaped.

> *Note:* To add text outside and above the table area, go to the first cell and place your cursor before any words that you may have input.
>
> Hit the up-arrow cursor key on your keyboard (the Table Control, see **Figure 13.5** in the last section), will blink. Now hit the Enter/Return key. The table should move down and a new paragraph marker should appear, giving you space above the table to type.

Figure 14.2: A table footnote appears at the bottom of a table.

Notes

15

Section II: Excel
The Excel Workspace and the
Mighty Format Cells Palette

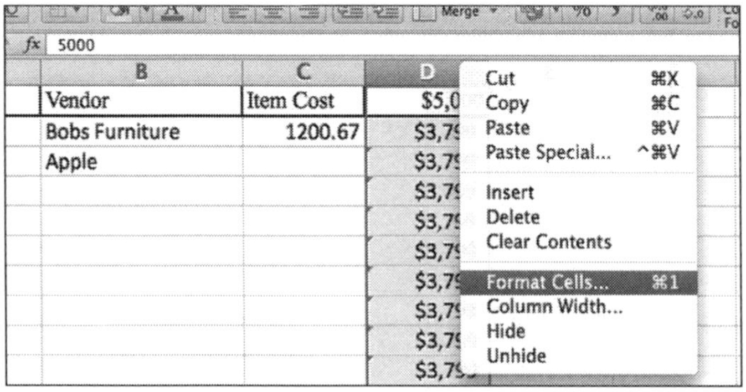

Figure 15.1: By right-clicking (Windows) or Command + clicking (Mac), a pop-up menu appears featuring a number of frequenty used commands or "moves" in Excel. In this case, the valuable "Format Cells" selection appears. Whenever Excel appears troublesome and it is not doing what you intend, use "Clear Contents" to start fresh. This is your "safety net" for now.

EXCEL IS THE SPREADSHEET and worksheet program that is the industry standard for a number of professions, including accounting and business management. A integral part of Microsoft Office, Excel has been wowing users and intimidating non-users since the mid-to-late 1980s.

Most people associate Excel with numbers-based work; yet Excel is not limited to spreadsheets and numbers: it can also produce graphics that can be exported and used in a PowerPoint presentation. In fact, Excel can be used in creating graphic organizers, databases, as well as Web pages (although not the best program for the Web).

The Excel workspace can be intimidating at first, especially to the beginner and those with limited experience. Another thing about Excel is that the math functions and how it works can appear to be different than most new user's experience with traditional ways of approaching math, mainly the pencil and paper. At the risk of sounding Zen-like, one of the challenges new Excel users face is learning how to "think with the program," rather than get Excel to work the way math is performed with a pencil and paper.

Another thing new Excel users may experience is the appearance that Excel sometimes "thinks" for itself and does things that the user does not wish to do. For example, a numerical value will be input into a cell, the user hits enter, and all of a sudden Excel converts that numerical value to a date or time. Understanding how to "fix" these problems and the shortcuts to get there can make learning Excel a lot easier.

We're first going to start with the Excel "workspace" and focus on the "Format Cells" palette. Gaining an understanding of these will make the Excel ride a lot smoother.

Clearing Contents of a Cell

For now, whenever something happens that appears (1) mystifying or (2) like Excel is "thinking on its own," always go to formatting popup menu. This can be achieved by right-clicking on the cell (Windows) or Control + Clicking (Mac). A popup menu will appear offering a number of choices (**Figure 15.1**, above): Cut (Command + X, Mac; Control + X, Windows), Copy (Command + C, Mac; Control + C, Windows), as well as "Insert…", "Delete…", Clear Contents, and so on.

Once again, for now, whenever something gets a little "hairy" or Excel appears to be doing things that you don't want it to do, select "Clear Contents" and try again. We'll get into explanations about this later; the "Clear Contents" option is just a safety valve for now (see **Figure 15.1**).

Format Cells

As you work in Excel, one of the most frequent tools you'll need to utilize will be the "Format Cells" feature.

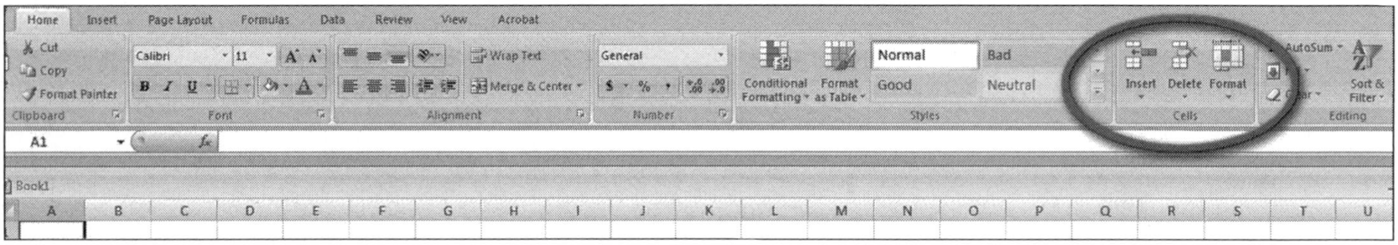

Figure 15.2: The Cells ribbon under the Home tab on the Windows version of Excel.

This feature brings you to the Format Cells palette, where a number of different properties can be applied to cells. The "Format Cells" feature can be accessed by right-clicking on the cell (Windows) or Control + Clicking (Mac) and selecting "Format Cells" in the popup menu. The Format Cells palette can also be accessed by hitting Control + 1 (Windows) or Command + 1 (Mac). It is also located in the Cells ribbon under the Home tab in the area labeled "Format" in Windows (see **Figure 15.2**).

Formulas and Getting Stuck

The first project we will be doing is a simple math problem involving subtraction. We will have to set up a formula. Sometimes, when an Excel user clicks on a cell that has a formula already applied, the user tries to click on other cells to get out of the cell and appears to be "stuck." If you click on a cell that has a formula, simply hit the Return or Enter key to get out of that cell. By clicking on other cells, you are only adding more cells to the formula that has been set.

The $5000 Bedroom

The Task

A generous uncle has given you a $5000 gift card to refurbish your bedroom. He says you can spend the money any way you please, as long as you purchase the following:

- Two cans of paint (let's say a standard bedroom size is 12' x 16')

- New Bed (Frame, box spring, mattress)

- Comforter/bedsheets/pillows

- Computer/laptop/mobile device such as a Tablet or iPad

- Desk and chair

Another condition your uncle placed on his gift of $5000 is that you have to spend all of the money within $1. After all, this makes sense in our ficticious world: af-

ter redeeming a $5000 gift card, you want to leave as little "leftover change" as possible.

You can also add on other items, such as a TV, a dock for an MP3 Player or iPod, etc. School supplies and other items—including MP3 files or music downloads—count as well.

You should use the Internet to figure out how much your dream bedroom is going to cost. Here are some web sites that sell bedroom items:

Ikea: http://www.ikea.com/ms/en_US/

Macy*s: http://www1.macys.com/index.ognc

HGTV: http://www.hgtv.com/hgtv/dp_bedrooms/

Home Depot: http://www.homedepot.com/

Lexington: http://www.lexington.com/index.cfm

Bob's Furniture: http://www.mybobs.com/

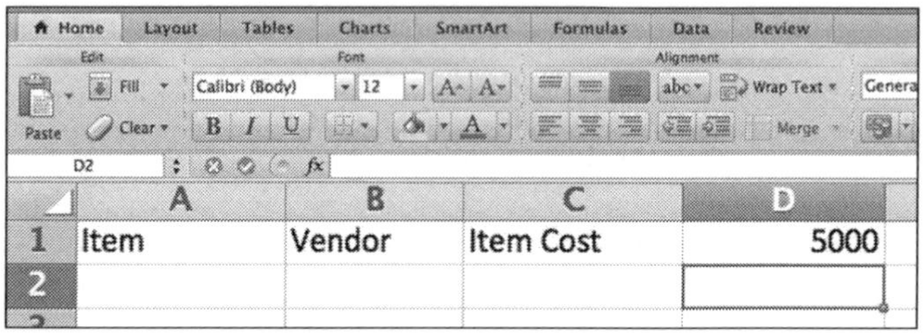

Figure 15.3: Setting up the columns for the $5000 bedroom. Skip the dollar sign for now—it may complicate things, such as Excel rounding off numbers when you don't want those numbers rounded off.

Your excel spreadsheet should be setup as follows:

By the way, a "vendor" is a store or retail outlet.

To let Excel do all the math for you, a formula is needed. Formulas in Excel are started by inputting an "=" sign, selecting the cells you want to effect, and then adding the desired mathematical operation. Once a formula is set in a column, it can be applied to all the subsequent cells in that column. By applying a formula to an entire column, Excel will update the information "automatically."

Setting Up a Formula: = The Equal Sign

This project will use subtraction mathematically; you are constantly subtracting the cost of each item from the 5000 dollars. To automate the process, go to the the D column in your Excel sheet beneath where the "5000" listed. Select the cell below (D,2) and input an "=" character. Next, click on the 5000 above (in the D1 column).

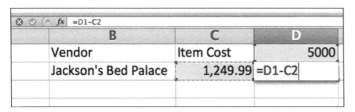

Figure 15.4: Inputting a formula. By hitting the "=" sign and then clicking on a cell that you wish to include in a mathematical operation, you are signaling to Excel that you wish to create a formula that can be applied to all data/information/numbers that are entered in the effected columns. Take note of the *fx* window above the "B" column; Excel displays formulas that are input in cells in this window. Also take note that once you enter a formula and you click back onto the cell where the formula exists, the only way to "get out" of that cell is to hit the Enter or Return key. Clicking on other cells will only add them to your formula and you'll appear "stuck."

The cell will look like this: =D1. Place a minus sign (hyphen on the keyboard) after the =D1 (see **Figure 15.4**).

Next, click on the cell next to your formula cell (C2). Your cell should now look like =D1-C2 (see **Figure 15.5** again). Now hit the "Enter/Return" key: this action executes the formula (in our case here, subtraction).

In the example provided here, we entered 1,249.99 as the cost of a bed from "Jake's Bed Palace." The value of 3,750.01 should appear in cell D2. Hover your cursor over to the lower right side of the cell where a dot appears. Your cursor should be a white cross, but as it intersects with the dot in the lower right corner, the cursor will turn black (see **Figure 15.5**).

Once the cursor is black, click-and-drag down to cell D-14; this will apply the formula to those cells in the D column. The 3,750.01 will repeat in each cell (see **Figure 15.6**).

fx	=D1-C2		
	B	**C**	**D**
	Vendor	Item Cost	5000
	Jackson's Bed Palace	1,249.99	3,750.01

Figure 15.5: When you cursor over to the lower-right corner "blue dot" of the cell where you input the formula, the cursor changes from a white cross to a black one, indicating that by clicking-and-dragging the cursor, the formula will be applied to the cells below in the column. Because we subtracted 1,249.99 from 5000, the remaining sum is 3,750.01. This number (3,750.01) will appear in the subsequent cells where the formula was applied. Each time you enter in a new item's price, the total will change. For example, say you enter a pillow case for $10, the number in the D column (5000) will automatically subtract 10 from 3,750.01 and the new total will appear (3,740.01).

		fx	=D1-C2	
A		**B**	**C**	**D**
m		Vendor	Item Cost	5000
d		Jackson's Bed Palace	1,249.99	3,750.01
				3,750.01
				3,750.01
				3,750.01
				3,750.01
				3,750.01
				3,750.01
				3,750.01
				3,750.01
				3,750.01
				3,750.01
				3,750.01
				3,750.01

Figure 15.6: Once the formula has been entered, it can be applied to the rest of the column by selecting the D2 cell, hovering your cursor to the lower right corner where the blue dot appears in the lower right corner, and then clicking-and-dragging downward to the desired end.

Once the formula has been applied, be sure to save the document. Now you're ready to go online and shop. After you have selected an item (bed, mattress, paint, computer, etc.), enter the item, the vendor (the place where you are buying the item), and the cost in the appropriate column.

Do not "round off" the cost; if an item is $1200.67, then input 1200.67 (again, leave the dollar sign out for now. Once you input a price for your items, those prices should automatically deduct from the 5000 column.

If the decimals are missing in the column or for some strange reason, Excel is automatically rounding off numbers (i.e., 12.99 is rounded to 13), then the cells need to be formatted to express the decimals. Click on the D column letter in order to highlight every cell in that column. Then right-click (Mac, Control + Click) on the D column and a popup menu will appear (see again **Figure 15.1**).

Select "Format cells." A dialogue box will appear. Make sure you are in the Number section along the top and you select "Custom" in the Category area. Scroll to where the section reads, "0.00." Select it and then click "OK." (**Figure 15.7**).

The decimals should now appear in the D1 column. Another area to check if Excel is doing "screwy" things is the "Currency" area. We'll look at each one of the areas in the Format Cells palette later.

One other thing: for now, we're going to keep things simple and avoid shipping costs. But in the "real world" of Internet purchasing, most vendors charge for delivery, whereas many give "free shipping" with a spending minimum.

Note: The symbols for simple math in Excel are - for subtraction, + for addition, / for division, and * (an asterisk, Shift + 8) for multiplication.

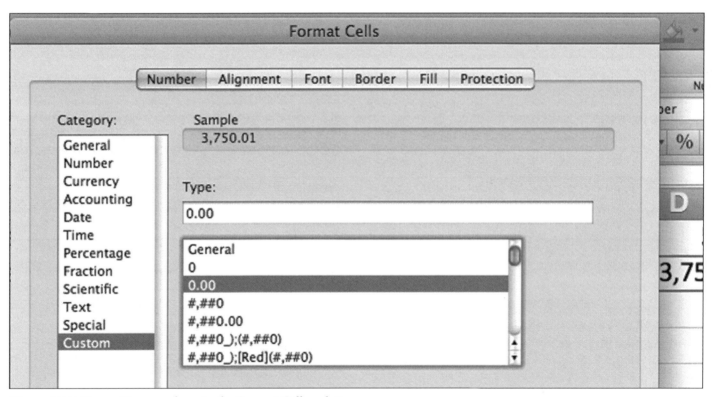

Figure 15.7: Formatting numbers in the Format Cells palette.

Notes:

16   Details on the Excel Workspace: A Reference Guide

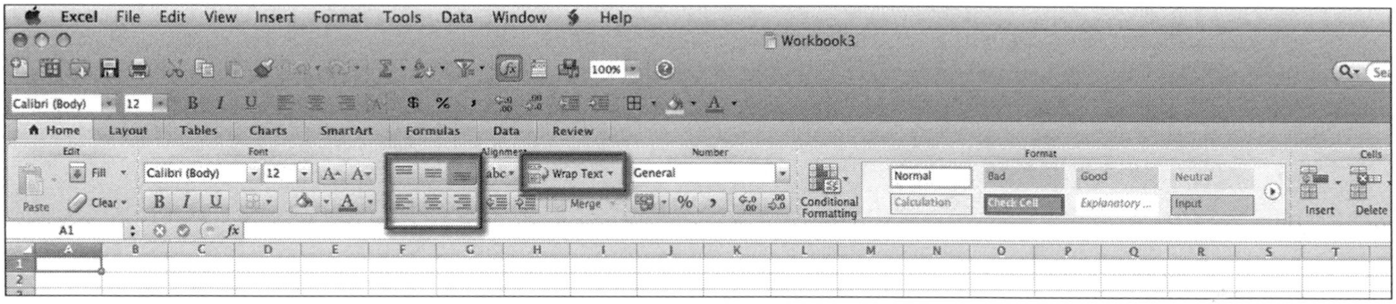

Figure 16.1: Excel on the Mac. Like the Windows version, there are a number of shortcuts to frequently used commands in the "Home" ribbon that are found in the other tabs (Layout, Tables, Formula, etc.). The toolbar can be customized in both the Mac and Windows versions.

THIS SECTION IS GOING to cover basic features and functions in the Excel "workspace." The descriptions here will be brief and hopefully serve as a reference section to which you can keep returning. Many of the concepts presented here will be repeated throughout the projects included here.

In the Windows platform, most of Excel's tools are already displayed in the ribbons and tabs. On the Mac, the setup is very similar but there are a few "adjustments" that need to be made. If you're a PC/Windows user, feel free to skip the next paragraph and go to the images and descriptions on the following pages.

On the Mac, the first thing to check for ease of use in Excel is to go to the "View" menu (see **Figure 16.2**), select "Toolbars" and make sure "Standard" and "Format-

ting" are checked off. By having the "Standard" and "Formatting" items checked, shortcuts to functions such as "save," "copy," "paste," as well as the "Sort" or "Auto Sum" tools are easy to access. The goal here is to cut down on the amount of time you spend clicking between ribbons (tabs).

Note: Because of a "bug" on some versions of Mac operating systems, some features such as the zoom box disappear. If both "Standard" and "Formatting" are checked off and the shortcuts do not appear, uncheck one of them and then re-check them again; usually, this will make them appear.

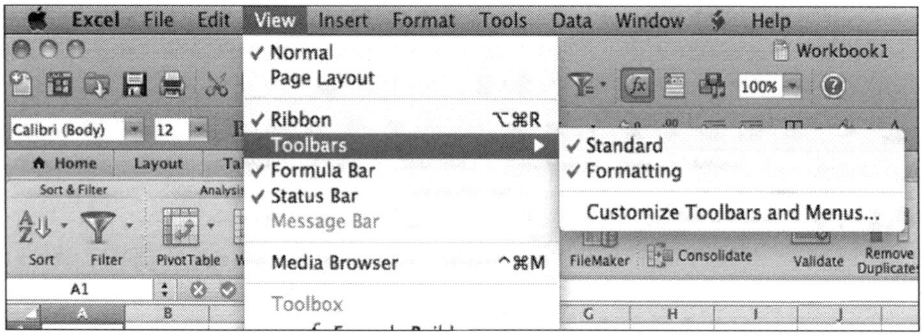

Figure 16.2: On the Mac version, ensuring that the "Standard" and "Formatting" toolbars are checked will keep many shortcuts available in the Home tab, which can also be edited and customized.

The Excel Workspace: Mac Home Ribbon

Once you have your Standard and Formatting bars in view, familiarize yourself with the "Ribbons." They are simple categories and each one is fairly self-explanatory. The first ribbon is "Home," which is the default in Excel, meaning that every time you launch Excel, the Home ribbon will appear first (see **Figure 16.3**). We'll be working primarily in the Home ribbon and its included shortcuts. In order to keep things simple, not every function in the Home Ribbon is going to be immediately addressed: just the basics first.

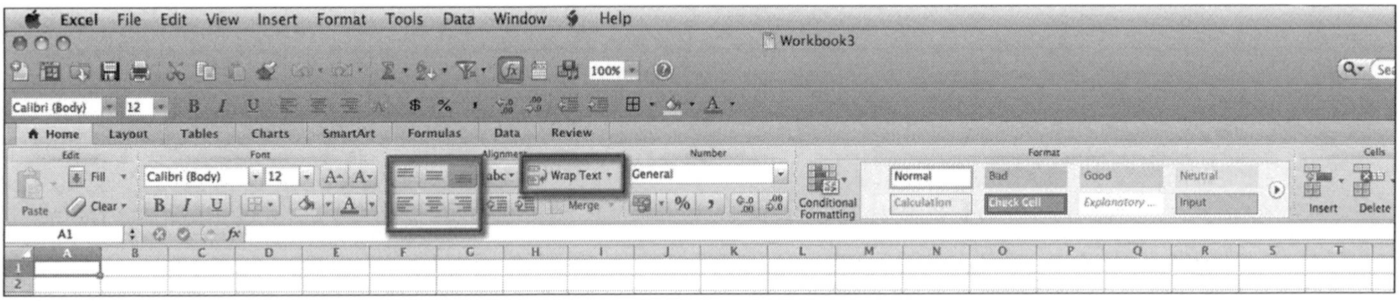

Figure 16.3: Home Ribbon. The "Home Ribbon" contains various editing functions similar to Microsoft Word: bolding, italicizing, font selection and size, and so on. Colorizing cells and fonts can also be achieved in the Home Ribbon. Some of the shortcuts on the Home Ribbon are similar to Microsoft Word's icons and layout, such as where font types and size are selected, the color of the text, bolding, italicizing and underlining. There are other features, such as rotating text within a cell, merging cells, colorizing cells, and alignment that will be focused on in the next few images.

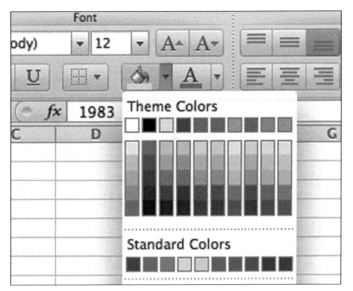

Figure 16.4: Paint bucket for filling cells with colors. Select a cell, row, or column and then click on the bucket. Border lines may disappear once a color fill has been added (make sure the effected cells are selected). To return the cell's borders, see below.

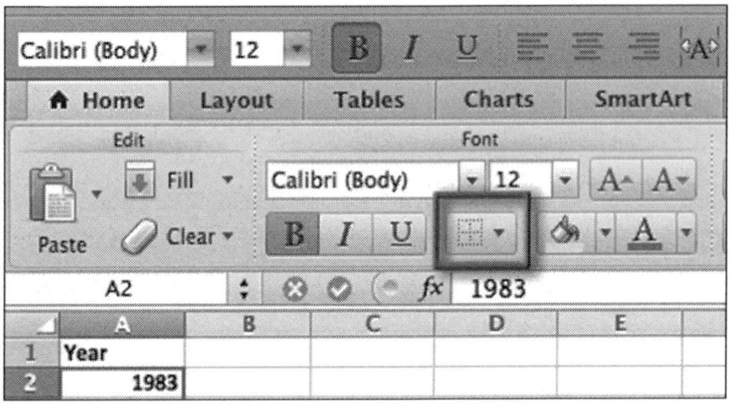

Figure 16.5: Applying borders to a selection, you can customize the borders by adding different line-widths and schemes (i.e., apply borders only to a series of cells on the outside while leaving inner borders clear, etc.). The cells you wish to alter or change must be selected before going into this tool. Using borders will ensure that the cell lines will print out.

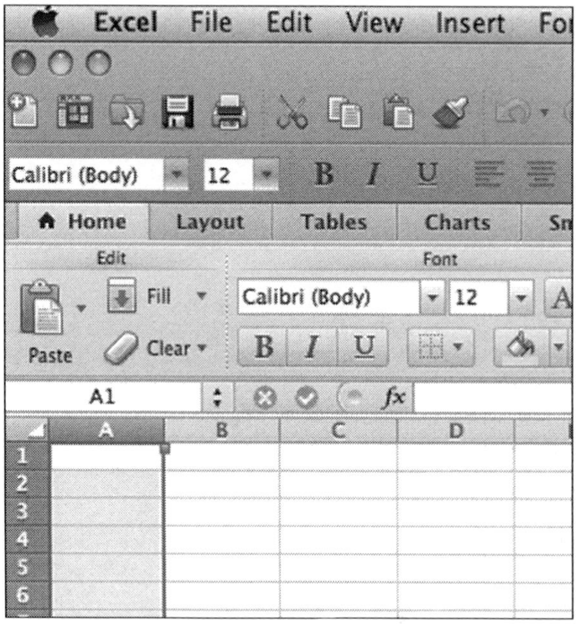

Figure 16.6: To apply formatting functions (fonts, color, rotation, alignment, etc.) to an entire column, click on the column letter.

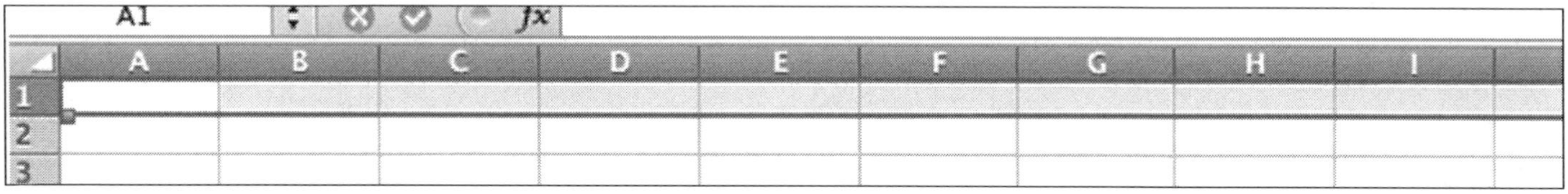

Figure 16.7: To apply formatting functions (fonts, color, rotation, alignment, etc.) to an entire row, click on the row number.

Figure 16.8: Just as cells, columns, and rows can be inserted or deleted by selecting "Control + 1" (Windows) or "Command + 1" (Mac) and then selecting the action from the popup menu, this can also be achieved by selecting the desired cells, columns or rows and applying the action through the icon pictured here.

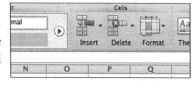

Figure 16.9: Each ribbon itself (Home, Layout, Tables, etc.) can be customized and edited by going to the upper right corner and looking for the "widget" or "gear" symbol, clicking on the down-arrow next to it and then selecting the appropriate checkoff boxes in the preferences palette.

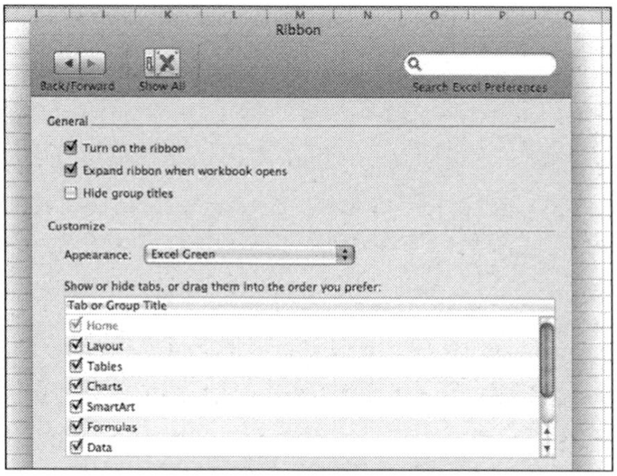

Figure 16.10: Ribbon preferences palette, where items that appear on the ribbon can be hidden or added, as well as color schemes.

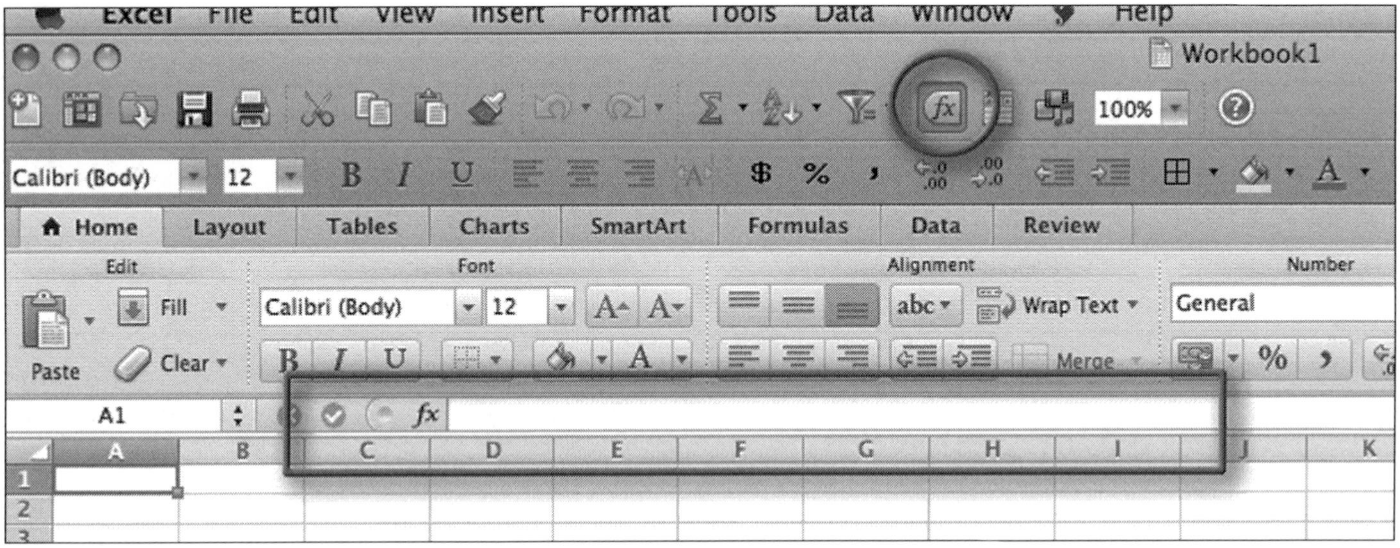

Figure 16.11: On the Mac, having the "Standard" and "Formatting" boxes checked off in the View>>Toolbars menu will lead you directly to frequently used operations, such as simple mathematical operations, sorting, and applying formulas. When the Formula Bar is selected (circled in this image), the Formula Bar is present right above the Column letters (highlighted by a rectangle). By having the Formula Bar exposed, a user can see every part of a formula being entered.

Suppose a user needs to multiply two values that were input into a cell and then divide the outcome by 2, and then add 10 to the outcome of that action (A x B ÷ 2 + 10). The formula that is being input into a cell will be displayed in the Formula Bar as well. This is also handy when a user clicks into a cell that already has a formula set in it; generally, most new Excel users will try to click into other cells in an attempt to escape the cell with the formula. Although this issue has been addressed earlier, it is important enough to repeat, especially for beginners.

By looking at the Formula Bar, the user can see that all he or she is doing is adding more cells to the existing formula. In other words, something is going wrong and the user is "stuck" in the cell. To get out of the cell, go into the Formula Bar's window, delete the accidental cells that were added to the formula and then hit the Enter/Return key.

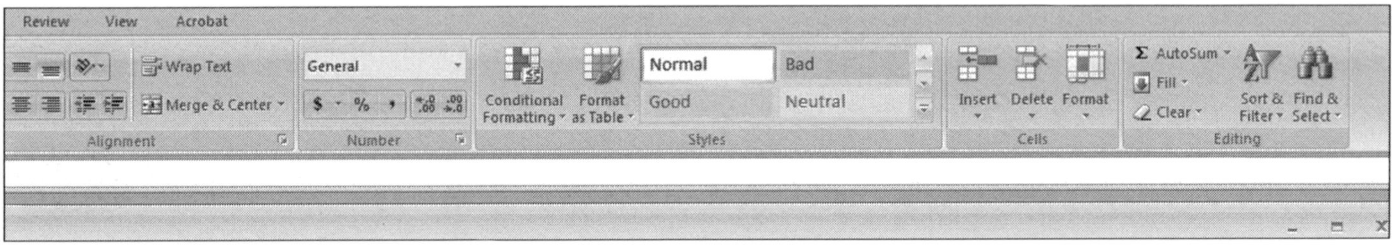

Figure 16.12: In Windows, the same shortcuts are also found in the Home ribbon. These shortcuts are also found in the Tables, Formula, and Data ribbons. The icons are the same on the Mac and in Windows; both versions give the user multiple paths to get to the same functions.

Figure 16.13: Shortcut to the Sort tool. This tool can place things in alphabetical or numerical order. It can go from lowest-to-highest ("Ascending") and from highest-to-lowest ("Descending"). Remember: you can only sort if you have the desired cells selected.

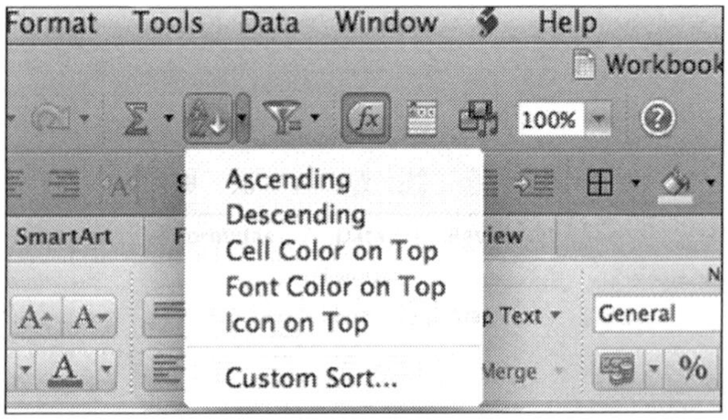

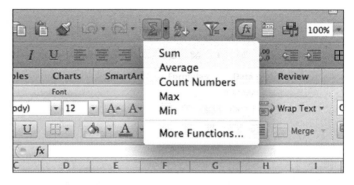

Figure 16.14: The AutoSum tool. The AutoSum tool is identified by the Greek character, the epsilon (Σ), or what some may call a "funky E." By selecting a row or column and then clicking on the epsilon, Excel will automatically add the numerical values that were selected. To perform other functions, such as getting an average, click on the down-arrow next to the epsilon and then apply the "Average" action. The AutoSum tool is also found in the Formulas ribbon.

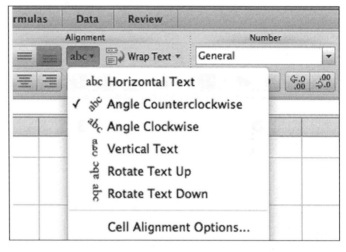

Figure 16.15: Text can be aligned, rotated, and moved within a cell in almost any direction.

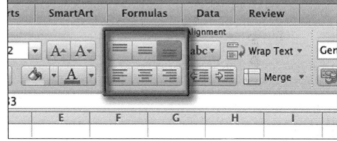

Figure 16.16: Text can be aligned left, center and right as well as north, center and south (relative to each cell).

Figure 16.17: Text can also be "shrunk" to fit the cell or the cell can be extended so it fits the text (Wrapped).

Figure 16.18: For spreadsheets that have an extensive amount of entries, you can "freeze" the category headers by going into the Layout tab (Mac) or the View tab (Windows) and click on the "Freeze Panes" icon. This will keep you category heads visible as you scroll down.

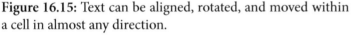

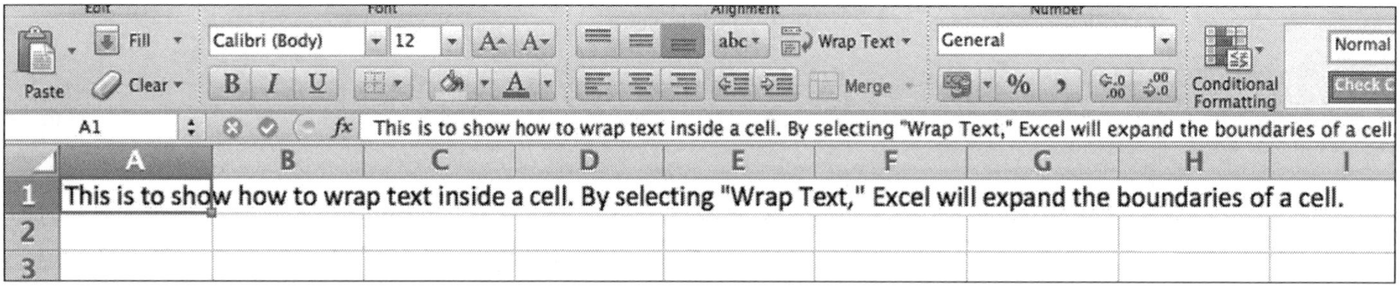

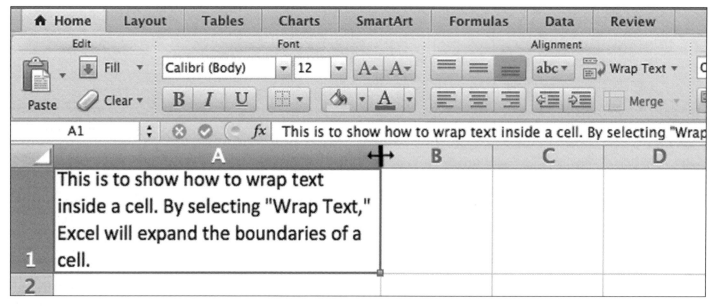

Figure 16.19: Sometimes extensive text needs to be input into cells in Excel. One way of fitting text into a cell is utilizing the "Merge Cells" feature but another way is "Wrap Text." By selecting "Wrap Text," the cell dimensions expand. Cell height and width can be adjusted by hovering your cursor to the right edge, waiting for the white-cross cursor to turn into a black line with arrows appearing and clicking-and-dragging. The text in the image depicts how it looks before "Wrap Text" is selected.

Figure 16.20: By hovering your cursor to the right of a cell, you can click-and-drag and reszie the cell and the textflow will fit the new dimensions. In the example pictured, the text will "push" the cell's boundaries, thereby increasing the cell's height. This also works horizontally or by the row, although adjusting row height is not recommnded: select "Wrap Text" and Excel will fit the text into the cell for you.

Figure 16.21: Merge cells. Whenever you want to merge two or more cells together, select them by either clicking-and-dragging or clicking on individual cells, holding down the shirt key while you click on other cells. and then selecting the Merge feature. This is especially useful if you need to add extensive text to an Excel spreadsheet.

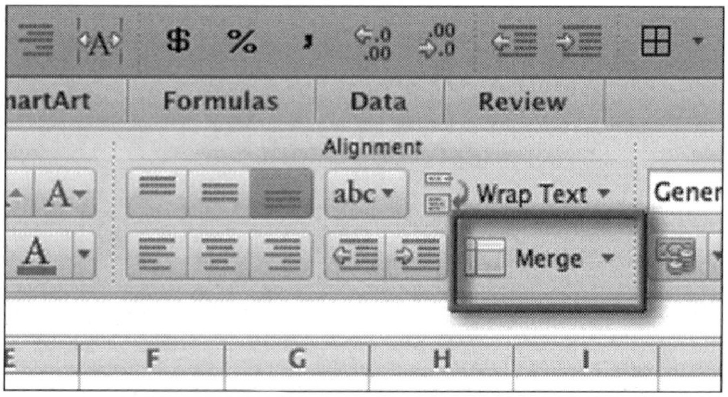

17 Plotting Charts in Excel: The Seven Deadly Sins at the Movies

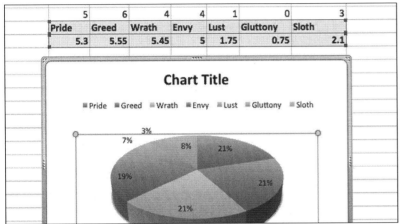

5	6	4	4	1	0	3
Pride	Greed	Wrath	Envy	Lust	Gluttony	Sloth
5.3	5.55	5.45	5	1.75	0.75	2.1

Figure 17.1: Quantifying the subjective: in this exercise, you'll assess movie villains, categorize them based on your opinion, and construct a pie chart to demonstrate your findings.

In this exercise, we're going to quantify, that is give numerical values, to textual analysis. Once the results are tallied, a chart will be built. This will give you an idea of how some charts and graphs, although rooted in facts, can easily be subjective (opinion-based) and then presented as "hard facts," a common approach the media and Federal Government take to convince people of an opinion or point of view that may or may not be valid.

The Task

You are hired by the Walt Disney Company to research common qualities among movie villains based on the Seven Deadly Sins. You're to review 20 of Walt Disney/Pixar's 50-plus animated movies, identify the main villain, and decide which of the Seven Deadly Sins dominates that character's personality. Based on your findings, you're to create a new villain, come up with a name and explain which three negative character traits your villain has. There are plenty of Web sites devoted to Disney villains that can be found by going into a search engine using the key words, "Disney Villians." Even if you did not see any of the Disney animated movies, there is enough material on the Web describing the movies that will give you a clear idea which one of the Seven Deadly Sins dominates the Disney villain in question.

Let's run through the Seven Deadly Sins: they are rooted in Greek, Roman, Jewish, and Christian traditions and were "codified" by the Roman Catholic Church. One need not be Catholic, Jewish, or Protestant to recognize these character traits as they are often portrayed in novels, short stories, poems, comic books, and movies and can readily be "secular" as well. Sometimes called "vices" or "Capital Sins," these traits are believed to be the root causes of human shortcomings and frailty. Most people who fall under these "Seven Deadly Sins" do not wake up and say, "I'm going to be greedy and angry today." Instead, they often arrive at these states of mind through a misguided understanding of the passions.

1. Pride

An excessively high opinion of oneself or one's importance is usually characterized as the wrong type of pride. Some claim that Pride is the "Queen" of the deadly sins; that it is the "root cause" of all the other maladies that humans experience through their actions.

In general, there are two types of "self love" or "pride." The first type of pride is healthy; it is the type that encourages us to become better people, whether it is striving to do better in school or at a job, learning a new skill,

Figure 17.2: Pride, the "queen" of the Seven Deadly Sins. Sometimes referred to as "vanity" or "narcissism," this form of pride is essentially "selfishness." Now taking "selfies" doesn't necessarily mean "narcissism," but it could be depending on the conditions.

or even mastering a sport or art. Being proud of one's accomplishments is not the same as being "prideful."

The second type of pride is the one that is detrimental and may lead to other excesses in areas, such as greed, wrath, or even lust. As the saying goes, "Pride comes before the fall" (or more accurately, "Pride goeth before destruction," made popular by British playwright William Shakespeare but derived from the Bible). For example, the person who is "greedy" feels that he or she deserves more than they need and ought not spare or even share what he or she has obtained.

The feeling of self-importance or an over-inflated view of oneself may result in the mistreatment of others which may ultimately backfire on the person with a "conceited" attitude who also falls prey to the other deadly sins. A man who thinks he is better than everyone may become envious when he sees another person with a better car or set of clothes. At the root of his jealousy is that he believes the other person is inferior and does not deserve to have the car or the "cool jacket." This type of thinking is often called "misdirected love," where the person does not make an effort to say, "Today I am going to be jealous," but simply assumes the attitude, "How dare he have a better house than me?"

The virtue that counters the sin of pride is known as **"Humility,"** which is a modest view of one's self. It is also called "humbleness" or "modest." This is known as keeping an even keel: don't allow yourself to get too high on your own accomplishments or too low on your failures (despair is directly related to the sin of pride).

2. Greed

Also called "avarice," greed is an intense desire for something, such as power, food, wealth, and fame. Now

don't misread this: there's nothing wrong with becoming a great scientist who becomes famous for discovering a cure for a disease or an athlete who accomplishes great feats on the field of play. Greed comes into play when it is mixed with the "bad" kind of pride and those admired skills and accomplishments are used for vainglory rather than service to others.

There are some philosophers who point out that those with such gifts have a duty, an "ought," to help those in need. Rather than have wealth confiscated by angry legions of revolutionaries, thieves, or a government pretending to do the work of charity, those who prosper with their talents, skills and gifts "ought" to help those less fortunate, especially with their "surplus" wealth. For example, there are many professional athletes who set up charitable foundations. Many private businesses have charitable foundations as well. This is not based on "Communism" or "socialism," but based in the American tradition of working hard and helping those less fortunate than ourselves, a system of "volunteerism."

For example, The Nobel Prize Foundation's prize money was left in abundance by Alfred Nobel, the chemist who invented dynamite back in 1896. It is through investments and interest earnings why his fortune was able to sustain itself for so long where the Foundation bestows about one million dollars a year to those who win in Medicine, Physics, Chemistry, Literature, Economics, and for peace. The total winnings for the categories is around six million dollars a year. So here is an example of fame and fortune being put to good use through the capitalist system, a system some people may describe as "greedy" and "unfair."

Figure 17.3: Greed is probably the most underscored of the Seven Deadly Sins in popular culture, especially in movies. Isn't it a bit funny how Hollywood moguls and actors live in tremendous mansions while lecturing the rest of us about greed?

Many religious traditions, from the Jewish, Catholic, Orthodox, and Protestant faiths, are all engaged in acts of charity and offer services to those who are not members of their respective congregations.

The virtue that counters greed is "**generosity**." But be careful with this virtue, as an excess of generosity can actually amount to pride, such as is the case with celebrities and politicians who stand in front of the news media and tell everyone how generous they are. In the case of celebrities, they earn their living mostly from young people, who get their money from their parents and pay celebrities by going to their movies or buying their music. If enough people buy the celebrities' products, the celebrities become very wealthy.

Many times celebrities lecture their fans to give to charities when those same celebrities have far more money than their fans. Some celebrities in the movie and music business even attack "corporations" for being greedy but meanwhile, these celebrities make millions of dollars working for huge media corporations. For celebrities in Hollywood and the music industry, it's very easy to preach from their mansions and penthouses.

Some politicians are a little different than celebrities. As celebrities earn much of their living from teenagers' allowance money, politicians earn their living from tax money. Once again, some politicians claim that they care about the poor and those who disagree with their solutions are "mean" and "greedy." Yet many politicians in Washington, D.C., are quick to prop themselves up as "caring" and "concerned" about the poor by attacking other politicians they claim "hate" or "don't care" about the poor. These politicians believe that using the power of the state to confiscate wealth is a form of charity. Most people know that coerced generosity is not charity. In other words, some politicians are very "generous" with other people's money.

3. Wrath

Also known as anger, this is a human emotion that is almost unavoidable. A person accidentally knocks you over in a supermarket, your first response may be anger. Yet you realize it was an accident, the person apologizes, and usually a mutual understanding follows. Anger is generally defined as "extreme rage" and an over-reaction to circumstances, but it can also be a "state of mind." When a person is known to be "angry," there is always the problem of pride underlying, as well as one of the other Seven Deadly Sins, such as Envy or Greed. Of all the Seven Deadly Sins, "anger" is the "combo sin," meaning that it usually has two or more of the other Deadly Sins.

The virtue that counters anger is "**patience**," or "**meekness**." This is characterized as the ability to be qui-

Figure 17.4: Anger is a human response to situations we feel are threatening or confrontational. It's not necessarily becoming angry, but our actions that count.

et and gentle. Those who exhibit patience can accept delay, trouble, or even insults without getting angry. To be sure, this may appear corny, especially the use of words like "meekness" and "gentle," yet being slow to anger or tolerating others' offenses can lead to a more peaceful life. Now this is not to say that one should embrace abuse or reject one's own dignity; having the "proper" sense of pride and self-respect will aid the person to cultivate "wisdom," which will help separate whether a given situation calls for self-defense or to laugh off ridiculous personal attacks.

4. Envy

(Jealousy): the resentful longing of other people's possession or talents. Here we have, once again, pride as the source of Envy: "How dare somebody else possess a talent that is greater than mine?" Or, "How dare somebody have a nicer pair of sneakers than me?" Instead of working hard at something such as mastering a sport, art, or skill, those who suffer from Envy generally have an over-exaggerated sense of how "great" they think they are and then become bitter when others seemingly surpass them.

Critics of Marxist-Communism state that Karl Marx's political, social, and economic system was greatly based on envy: stoking resentment from the working class to divide it from the middle- and upper-classes. Oddly enough, many of the leaders of Communist movements, such as Vladimir Lenin in Russia and Fidel Castro in Cuba, came from the upper-middle class (Lenin was a lawyer, as was the Jesuit-educated Castro). In fact, Karl Marx did not come from the "working class," but was the son of a lawyer. Marx's partner, Friedrich Engels, was a wealthy industrialist.

Communism also seems to appeal to many in the "non-wealth producing professions," such as some

Figure 17.5: It's easy to become jealous of others, especially those who we think have something that we want. This is especially common with people who earn less money than those who earn a lot of money, which can also be considered a combination of greed and envy.

members of the academic and entertainment worlds. It is common to hear some college professors and school teachers complain that doctors, athletes, rock stars, and lawyers earn more money than educators while extolling the virtues of "economic equality." Does this mean they believe all jobs should be paid the same wage? And since there are many in the education system who ardently bemoan and loathe capitalism, does this mean they are going to reject their pension plans, many of which rely on investments and dividends?

Following the plea for "economic equality," does a group of five teenagers with musical instruments constitute a "rock band," so therefore, they should earn an equal amount of money as the Rolling Stones?

Should we start paying transplant surgeons the same amount of money as fry cooks? What do celebrities, activists, and politicians mean when they say "economic equality?" Are they saying that the woman starring in a local community play should be paid the same as the starlet in a blockbuster Hollywood movie?

These are all classic examples of "envy" and, in many cases, mixed with anger and pride. To be sure, those who are envious generally assume that the rock star, lawyer, or doctor did not have to work too hard to reach their level of accomplishment, which in many cases is untrue.

The virtue that counters Envy is "**Charity**," which is the voluntary giving of help, usually in the form of mon-

ey, to those in need. Being charitable also means sometimes stating what some people do not want to hear.

5. Lust

Lust may be summed up as having a "very strong sexual desire" that eventually objectifies a person. Lust is the opposite of love in that it dehumanizes both people involved. Throughout the history of humanity, there have always been people who attempt to justify lust under the guise of "love," in which the procreative act becomes a manipulative and deceiving act rather than an act of love. Today, the manipulative act has been celebrated in pop culture where the banal is celebrated and true love is treated as something "prude" or "ignorant."

Think of "lust" in this way: a steak knife has a purpose and that is to cut food. When a steak knife is being used in its correct way, then it is a "good:" the steak knife is assisting the person in nourishing the body. Yet when that same steak knife is being used to mug people, then it is not being used for its original intended purpose.

In the natural order of life, all things are always evolving to a higher or greater consciousness. The infant is not born to remain an infant forever; he or she will develop into a "toddler," then a "child" (although both are technically "children"), move onto adolescence, then adulthood, and then eventually become elderly. The point here is that in most cases, human beings are not born to be infants and are expected to grow and develop. The same can be said about the human sex drive: what is the point of what is commonly called "sex" today?

In many popular Hollywood movies and pop songs, there seems to a celebration of objectifying people to

Figure 17.6: For some strange reason, "lust" has become the most controversial of the deadly sins in the past 30 or 40 years. Part of the reason for this is the mainstreaming of pornography and its easy availability through the Internet. Lust is essentially the objectification of a person and yes, two "consenting adults" can objectify one another.

satisfy the sexual impulse, which as everyone knows, is found in animals and humans alike. Some people are under the impression that human beings are simply over-developed animals and cannot control these impulses so therefore, anything that takes place between consenting adults is moral.

Other people believe that although human beings may be "overdeveloped animals," they do possess an intellect and the ability to over-ride their passions, unlike most animals when it is mating season (it has been noted that some animal species may be more selective when it comes to mating than some human beings). The question of lust becomes muddled when people justify sex under the pretense of "love" or that like animals, some people are born with a genetic mutation and they simply cannot use their intellect to over-ride their impulses.

The question regarding "sex" is, what is its ultimate goal? Is it simply a recreational or athletic activity people use to make themselves feel better or to satisfy their "animal" cravings, or is there a higher order to sex? Is sex an end unto itself?

The virtue that counters "lust" is "**chastity**," which has been ridiculed endlessly by pop culture, Hollywood and/or the pornography industry, some pseudo intellectuals who have jobs as college professors and "educators," as well as activists who feel strongly about being "sex positive." Yet chastity, properly understood, is not "prudery," with which many pseudo-intellectuals confuse "chastity." *Prudery* is really associated with *sanctimony*, which is a form of "bad" **pride** that a person is morally superior to others.

Unlike prudishness or sanctimony, chastity is about showing respect for oneself and allowing the intellect to control the passions. The media and academic spheres often praise those who display the virtue of generosity or moderation yet attack those who profess chastity as being "extreme," "judgmental," and "ungenerous." The virtue of chastity also demonstrates respect for others to the point where there may very well be a sexual desire, but the person who respects others and values people as thinking human beings is not willing to use other people in order to satisfy his or her own selfish, if not greedy, desires. Lust can also take the form of an object (such as the phrase, "A lust for power and wealth").

6. Gluttony

This vice is generally associated with "habitual greed or excessive, inordinate eating." Let's first make a distinction between the person who suffers from a medical condition often called "obesity" and discuss the human will as it relates to gluttony. The glutton will eat for the sake of luxury rather than nourishment. It is one thing to enjoy a piece of cake here and there, it is another to devour an

Figure 17.7: Gluttony is, more or less, the objectification of food. It's one thing to enjoy a celebratory feast or nourish oneself, it's quite another for eating for the sheer pleasure of eating.

entire cake. Gluttony usually comes with greed and lust, although one can simply be a pure glutton. The cake, in and of itself, is not evil nor is it "bad" to enjoy a piece of cake. In fact, celebrating the baker's art with friends and family is a "good" and indeed a virtue.

Gluttony comes into play when food is no longer thought of as a source of nourishment and pleasure, but pleasure first and foremost. This is not to imply that those who enjoy a good meal are acting unethically or immorally unless they say, "I am nourishing myself." This is to state that using food as a means unto itself, just like sex, is unethical.

Drunkeness and drinking to excess also fall under the gluttony category.

The virtue used to counter gluttony is **Moderation,** which falls under Aristotle's admonition, "All things in moderation." This phrase is sometimes taken out of context. Aristotle defines some human actions that can never be moderate, such as murder. We certainly don't accept as an excuse, "But she only murdered one person, whereas there are some murderers who killed ten people."

7. Sloth

Sloth is generally associated with laziness and is defined as a reluctance to work or make an effort. Of all the vices, sloth may be the most subtle and abstract: most of us think we are "educated," especially by virtue of us going to school and college. Although this may be true, many times information is presented by educators and the media where facts are omitted. Just a look at any history textbook will demonstrate how partial stories are told to make various historical figures or events look "evil" or "good."

Many times an educator may be too intellectually slothful to fact-check a textbook and somehow "trusts" what has been published. Although the teacher has not intended to maliciously spread ignorance, by virtue of her intellectual sloth she is unknowingly spreading half-truths and distortions. This is one reason why when so many students enter college, their professors advise them to "forget" what they learned in high school because everything they learned was "half-true" or untrue. Yet there are many instances where ideologically-driven college professors appear more interested in imposing their beliefs on their students as well and present the "facts" of a subject so it fits their own biases. In many cases, students feel coerced to write or say what they think the professor wants or else they may receive a bad grade.

Intellectual sloth is not only found in schools and colleges, it is also found in real life. For example, when you get your driver's license, it is up to you to know and understand the rules of the road. Should a police officer pull you over and you receive a moving violation ticket, you cannot offer the excuse that you "didn't know." As the old saying goes, "Ignorance of the law is no excuse."

Worse than a ticket is the potential for serious legal trouble after receiving your license: Reckless, distracted, or aggressive driving can result in charges of vehicular homicide or manslaughter should another person die in an auto accident in which you are involved. The charge of manslaughter, although less than homicide, is still serious enough (manslaughter is killing another person without malice or intention). Claiming that you "didn't know" or did not "intend" to hurt anyone by driving 50 miles-per-hour in a 30 miles-per-hour zone is not going to help you, nor will it prevent the expensive legal fees that are usually involved in such matters.

Sloth is also characterized by plain "laziness." The student who does not work to her full potential is slothful. The son or daughter who doesn't help with chores around the house is slothful.

Another characteristic of sloth is "despair." This is a total loss of hope. For example, many times students will fall behind a class, give up and accept they just "aren't good" at the subject. Although that may be the case—a particular subject may indeed be a weak area for a student—that does not mean the student ought to quit. Instead, the student should seek extra help and at least go down fighting.

The virtue that counters sloth is "**zeal**." Having zeal means to have enthusiasm for a pursuit. Although there are some school subjects that are boring and seemingly "useless," it is still necessary to have "zeal" towards them so one can learn as much about the world as possible.

There is also a derivative of "zeal," the word "zealot." Usually this word is used to describe a fanatic who is uncompromising. In many instances, the zealot is in a state of pride and many of his attributes are similar to

Figure 17.8: While there's nothing wrong with laying on the couch and texting your friends for a break, there is something wrong with spending four or five hours doing this, especially when you have homework or other priorities. Sloth can also be a state of despair, when a person completely quits and loses all hope.

the "prude" or "sanctimonious" person who has an over-inflated sense of himself or the cause he portends to be important.

As noted earlier, sloth is the most subtle of the Seven Deadly Sins. At its root is "despair," what some modern thinkers call "depression" or pessimism. In many instances, those under the spell of sloth have given into the idea that certain things are hopeless and have, more or less, embraced a spirit of defeatism and negativity. To paraphrase another cliche, it's better to go down swinging than to passively accept that you are doomed to failure.

The Task: Rating Villains

Below is a list of Disney/Pixar animated movies. Go onto the Internet and look up the movies and villains. A useful search phrase is "Disney Villains." The Walt Disney Website also has a section devoted to their villains, but you may use third party Websites run by fans, etc..

Some movies may have more than one villain so pick the villain you feel is the "lead" villain. In some cases, there may not be an evil villain in the movie but a "rival." Although there is a difference between an "evil villain" and a "rival," many times, rivals possess the same character traits found in the Seven Deadly Sins.

Also, some of these movies are about a main character who's own worst enemy is him- or herself; the character has to overcome a flaw or weakness. In these cases, it's acceptable to list the character struggling with a flaw as a "villain" since in many instances in movies and in real life, we are sometimes our own worst enemies.

1. *Snow White and the Seven Dwarfs*/Evil Queen
2. *Pinocchio*/Mr. Stromboli
3. *Dumbo*/The Clowns
4. *The Adventures of Ichabod and Mr. Toad*
   Mr. Winkie
   Brom Bones
5. *Cinderella*/Lady Tremaine
6. *Peter Pan*/Captain Hook
7. *Lady and the Tramp*/Si and Am
8. *Sleeping Beauty*/Maleficent
9. *101 Dalmatians*/Cruella de Vil
10. *The Sword in the Stone*/Madame Mim
11. *The Jungle Book*/Shere Khan
12. *The Aristocats*/Edgar the Butler
13. *Robin Hood*/Prince John
14. *The Rescuers*/Madame Medussa
15. *The Fox and the Hound*/Amos Slade
16. *The Black Cauldron*/The Horned King
17. *The Great Mouse Detective*/
    Professor Ratigan
18. *Oliver & Company*/Sykes
19. *The Little Mermaid*/Ursula
20. *The Rescuers Down Under*/ Percival McLeach
21. *Beauty and the Beast*/Gaston
22. *Aladdin*/Jafar
23. *The Lion King*/Scar
24. *Pocahontas*/Governor Ratcliffe
25. *The Hunchback Of Notre Dame*/Frollo
26. *Hercules*/Hades
27. *Mulan*/Shan Yu
28. *Tarzan*/Clayton
29. *The Emperor's New Groove*/Yzma
30. *Atlantis: The Lost Empire*/Lyle Rourke
31. *Lilo And Stitch*/Captain Gantu
32. *Treasure Planet*/Captain Silver
33. *Brother Bear*/Denahi
34. *Cars*/Chick Hicks
35. *Finding Nemo*/Marlin or Darla
36. *Toy Story*/Sid Phillips
37. *Toy Story 2*/Al McWhiggin
38. *Toy Story 3*/Lotso
39. *The Incredibles*/Syndrome
40. *Ratatouille*/Chef Skinner
41. *Monsters, Inc.*/Randall
42. *A Bug's Life*/Hopper
43. *Dinosaur*/Kron
44. *Home on the Range*/Alameda Slim
45. *Meet the Robinsons*/DOR-15
46. *Chicken Little*/The Aliens
47. *WALL-E*/Auto
48. *Bolt*/The Director
49. *Up*/Charles Muntz
50. *The Princess and the Frog*/Doctor Facilier
51. *Tangled*/Mother Gothel
52. *Wreck-It Ralph*/Turbo
53. *Frozen*/Hans
54. *Big Hero 6*/Robert Callaghan

Step -by-Step Instructions

Open Excel, create a new workbook and save the file appropriately and in the correct area. Select 20 of the 54 movies listed here and input the name of the movie in column A. Identify the movie's villain and input the names into column B. In columns C through I, enter the Seven Deadly sins as column heads (be sure to apply bold text to the column headers by clicking on Row 1 and selecting the bold icon).

Now evaluate each character to decide which of the Seven Deadly Sins dominates that character. Use a scale of 0 to 7, with "0" representing that this deadly sin is not found in the character and "7" representing that that sin dominates the character. Numbers 1-6 would indicate that these sins are "less" or "more" than the dominating sin (for an example, see **Figure 17.9**).

Although the Seven Deadly Sins are objective truths and have been observed in human beings throughout history, how you apply them to characters is based on your judgement. For example, some people may think the dominant deadly sin in Lady Tremaine is envy,

	A	B	C	D	E	F	G	H	I	J
1	**Movie Name**	**Villain**	**Pride**	**Greed**	**Wrath**	**Envy**	**Lust**	**Gluttony**	**Sloth**	
2	Snow White And The Seven Dwarfs	The Evil Queen	6	5	4	7	2	0	3	
3	Pinocchio	Mister Stromboli	4	6	3	2	3	5	2	
4	Dumbo	The Ringmaster	3	7	4	2	4	6	5	
5	Cinderella	Lady Tremaine (Evil Step Mother)	6	5	4	7	2	0	3	
6	Peter Pan	Captain Hook	4	6	7	5	1	0	2	
7	Sleeping Beauty	Maleficent	6	5	6	7	2	0	1	

Figure 17.9: Your worksheet should look something like this. Try to avoid rating two of the Seven Deadly Sins with the same number.

whereas others may argue pride. Determining which of the Seven Deadly Sins dominates a character is debatable and a matter of opinion.

The Autosum Tool Σ

Once you have completed rating the villains, "average out" the column utilizing the Autosum Tool (Σ); (see **Figures 17.10** and **17.11**). The Autosum tool's options are capable of adding, averaging, and counting total sums of numbers within a column (or row). First, select the number ratings you input into the Pride column (Column C) by clicking on the C2 cell, holding down the shift key, and then selecting the number in cell C21. The numbers in the column should be highlighted. This can also be accomplished by selecting cell C2 and clicking-and-dragging your cursor down to cell C21.

Figure 17.10: On the Mac version, the AutoSum tool appears in the Home Ribbon..

Figure 17.11: On the Windows version, the AutoSum tool also appears in the Formulas Ribbon..

Once you have calculated the averages for each deadly sin, select row 22, right-click (Control + click on the Mac). Select "Insert" from the popup menu (see **Figure 17.12**). A blank row will appear in row 22 (with the aver-

Figure 17.12: Rows and columns can be deleted or inserted by right-clicking (Control + clicking for Mac).

ages now appearing in row 23). Select row 1 and Copy the category headers (Pride, Greed, Envy, etc.), right-click (Windows) or Control + click (Mac), select "Copy." A marquee ("marching ants") will appear around the row.

Right-click (Windows) or Control + click (Mac) on row 22 and select "Paste." The category headers should appear in row 22. High-light only the category headers from Cells C22 to I22 and C23 and I23 (see **Figure 17.13**).

With both areas still highlighted, go into the Insert Ribbon (Windows) or the Chart Ribbon (Mac), and select the 3D Pie Chart option. You'll notice that the pie chart appears and the Seven Deadly Sins are broken down according to the averages that you've assigned. Still needed is a pie chart title. There are a few different ways to do this.

Adding a Chart Title

The simplest way to add a table title, as well as percentage breakdowns of the pie chart, is to go to Quick Layouts in the Insert tab (Windows) or the Charts tab (Mac) and then double-clicking on the chart.

In the Windows version of Excel, there's a "Design" tab that appears once you double-click on the pie chart. For this project, we want to select the option that places

15	Hunchback of Notre Dame	Frollo	7	5	6	4	5	0	0
16	Hercules	Hades	6	5	7	5	1	0	0
17	Tarzan	Clayton	5	6	7	4	2	0	2
18	The Emperor's New Groove	Yzma	5	6	7	5	0	0	3
19	The Incredibles	Syndrome	6	5	7	5	0	0	3
20	Toy Story	Sid Phillips	5	4	7	6	0	0	3
21	Ratatouille	Chef Skinner	5	6	4	4	1	0	3
22	Movie Name	Villain	Pride	Greed	Wrath	Envy	Lust	Gluttony	Sloth
23			5.3	5.55	5.45	5	1.75	0.75	2.1
24									

Figure 17.13: Highlight only the category names and the average results and then go into the Charts ribbon (Mac) or Insert ribbon (Windows) and select the 3D Pie Chart option.

the Chart Title and the chart legend (that's the Seven Deadly Sins categories with the little colored boxes next to them) and also breaks down the information by percentage (see **Figure 17.14**). On some versions of Excel, this option is called "Layout 2." To edit the text, just click on the placeholder text (Chart Title) and input "Seven Deadly Sins and Disney Villains."

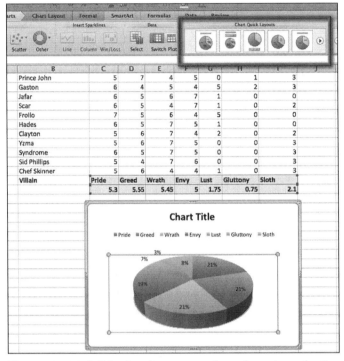

Figure 17.14: With the chart area selected, go into the Insert area (Windows) or the Chart area (Mac) and browse through the options in the Quick Chart area. On the PC, a Design tab will appear when you select the pie chart. Click where it says "Chart Title" and input the name.

Landscaping

Finally, let's landscape the document and input a running head. To landscape an Excel document, go to the Layout tab, select "Orientation," and choose the Landscape option (see **Figure 17.15**).

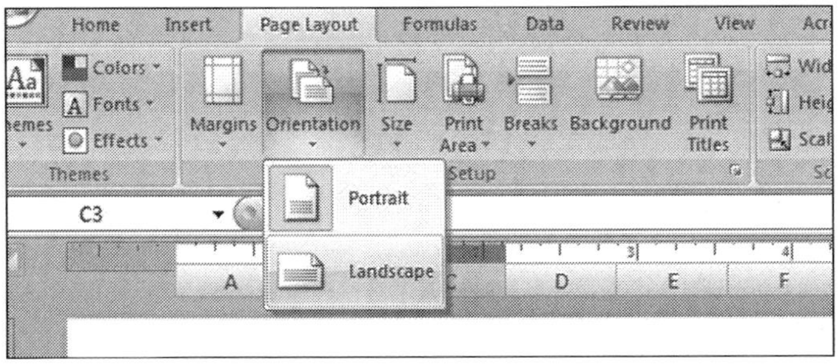

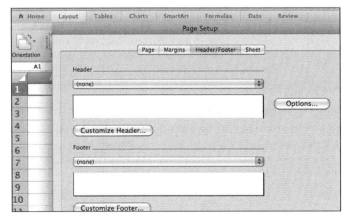

Figure 17.15: Look for the Orientation icon in the Page Layout tab to landscape or set your Excel document.

Headers

To input a running head on the Windows version, click on the Insert tab and select the Header & Footer icon (**Figure 17.16**, Windows; **Figure 17.17**, Mac). Three input areas will appear at the top of your worksheet area. In the left area, input your name. In the center, type in "Seven Deadly Sins and Disney Movies." In the right section, input the date (spell out the month, please).

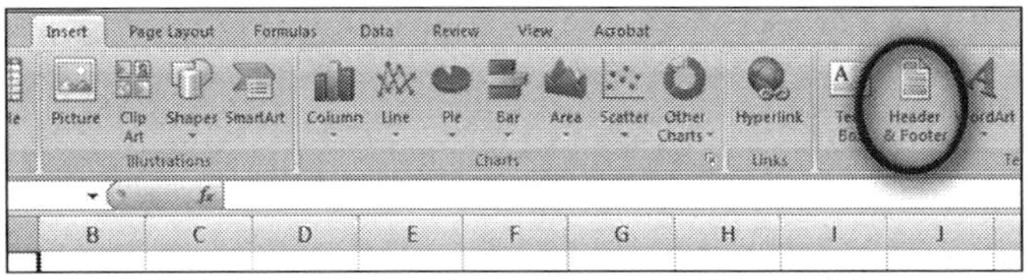

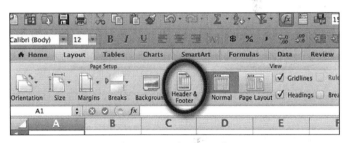

Figure 17.16: In Windows, the Header & Footer icon is located in the Insert tab.

Figure 17.17: On the Mac, the Header & Footer icon is found in Layout, but it can also be accessed by going to the View menu. The Header is very useful especially when you need to print out an Excel spreadsheet.

Inputting a running head on the Mac is one of the few areas where both platforms react differently. Click on the Layout tab and select "Header & Footer" (see **Figure 17.18**). A dialog box that reads "Page Setup" will appear.

Figure 17.18: On the Mac, click on the Customize Header option.

Select the Customize Header button and another dialog box named "Header" will appear (**Figures 17.19**).

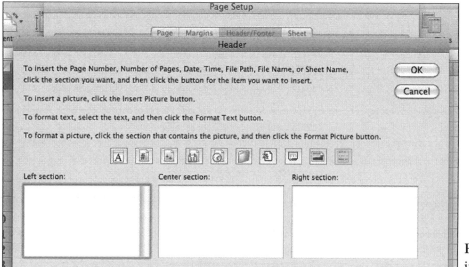

Figure 17.19: On the Mac, now you can input a running head in each section.

Input your name in the left section. In the center, type in "Seven Deadly Sins and Disney Movies." In the right section, input the date. The Header and Footer dialog box can also be accessed by going into the View menu on the Mac.

Movie Critic: Rating the Movies

Now that we've been able to determine which of the Seven Deadly Sins are the most used in Disney/Pixar movie villains, let's rate the movies. Copy the movie list from Column A, add a worksheet by double-clicking on the worksheet tabs at the bottom of the Excel workspace area and name it "Movie Ratings." Name B1 "Four Stars," C1 "Three Stars," D1 "Two Stars," and E1, "1 Star." Rate each movie according to each column's number: if you think *Snow White* is a four-star movie, then put the number 4 in the Four Star column. If you think *101 Dalmatians* is a two-star movie, then put the number 2 in the Two Stars column.

When you are finished rating the movies, select the numeric values in each column and then add them using the AutoSum tool (Σ). Once again, right-click (Windows) or Control + click (Mac) on Row 22 and Insert a blank row between Row 21 and Row 22 by right-clicking (Control + click, Mac) on Row 21 and selecting "Insert" from the popup menu (see **Figure 17.20**). Copy and paste the categories listed in Row 1 into Row 22. The addition results should be in row 23. Select Cells B22 through B23

Movie Name	Four Stars	Three Stars	Two Stars	One Star
Snow White And The Seven Dwarfs	4			
Pinocchio	4			
Dumbo	4			
Cinderella	4			
Peter Pan	4			
Sleeping Beauty	4			
101 Dalmatians		3		
The Jungle Book	4			
The Aristocats		3		
Robin Hood		3		
Beauty And The Beast		3		
Aladdin		3		
The Lion King		3		
Hunchback of Notre Dame			2	
Hercules		3		
Tarzan				1
The Emperor's New Groove	4			
The Incredibles	4			
Toy Story	4			
Ratatouille		3		
Movie Name	**Four Stars**	**Three Stars**	**Two Stars**	**One Star**
	40	24	2	1

Figure 17.20: Your movie rating data should look something like this.

to E22 and E23. Now go to the Insert tab (Windows) or Charts tab (Mac) and select the 3D Column option under the Column chart icon (**Figure 17.21**).

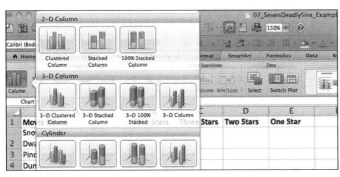

Figure 17.21: With cells B22 to E23 select, go into the Column chart icon and select 3-D Clustered Column.

Editing the Text Legend on a Chart

Double-click on the word "Series 1," which should be located on the right side of the column chart (see **Figure 17.22**). A "Format Legend" dialog box will appear (see **Figure 17.23**). Go to the Placement area in the dialog box and click on the Top radial button. The phrase "Series1"

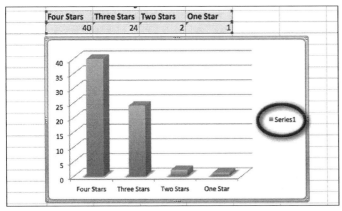

Figure 17.22: Look for the "Series 1" to appear on your chart.

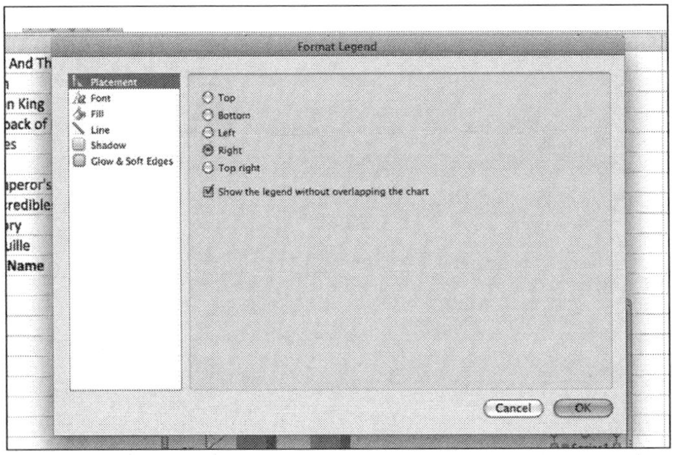

Figure 17.23: The Format Legend dialog box.

will appear at the top of the chart. There are other options in the "Format Legend" dialog box, such as artistic or graphic designs like drop shadows, lines, and fills, but we'll refrain from these for now.

Click the "OK" button on the lower right side of the "Format Legend" dialog box and now the "Series 1" will appear centered above the columns. Now click off the chart and select it by clicking on the chart's edge. Right-click (Windows) or Control + click (Mac) and choose "Select Data" from the popup menu (see **Figure 17.24**). A dialog box named "Select Data Source" will appear (see **Figure 17.25**). With Series 1 selected in the Series area,

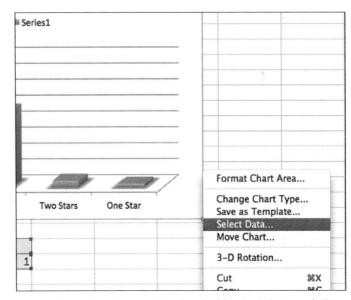

Figure 17.24: To change the placeholder text that reads "Series 1" to a chart title, right-click (Control + click, Mac) on the chart's edge and choose "Select Data" from the popup menu.

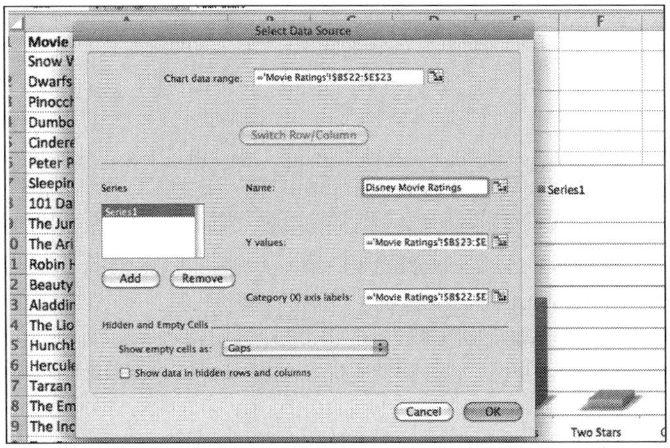

Figure 17.25: On the Mac, by entering text in the Name field of the Select Data Source dialog box you can change the name from "Series1" to a customized chart name.

input "Disney Movie Ratings" in the Name area (Mac).In Windows, select "Series 1," then click on "Edit" and input "Disney Movie Ratings" (see **Figure 17.26**). Then hit the OK button on the lower right corner of the Select Data Source dialog box. The chart is now customized (see **Figure 17.27**).

A New Villain

Create a new tab and name it "New Villain." Select cells A1 through F6, merge them, and briefly describe and name your new villain. Please indicate which of the Seven Deadly Sins are prevalent in the character. Remember your "Merge Cells" icon is in the Home ribbon. Don't forget to "Wrap" your text (right above "Merge Cells.").

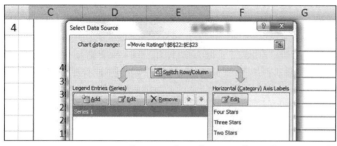

Figure 17.26: In Windows, select "Series1" in the Legends Entries area. Next, click on the "Edit" button. Input the new name.

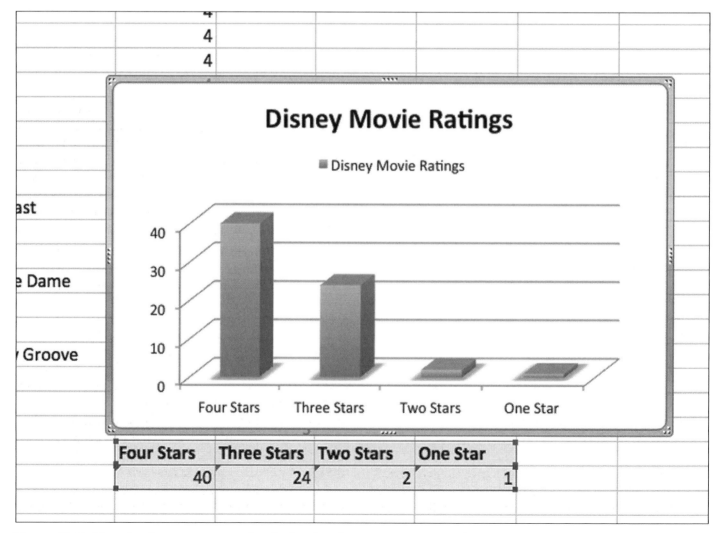

Figure 17.27: Now the chart is customized and related to the graphic story or information that is being presented..

18 SmartArt Charts: Planning Your Million Dollar Dream Home

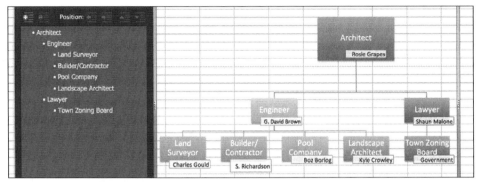

Figure 18.1: "Smart Art" is a feature found in Microsoft Word, PowerPoint, and Excel. It can be used to create items such as graphic organizers and can be used to organize data.

So you made a gazzilion dollars because you invented a new type of cell phone, developed a form of renewable energy, wrote a hit song, or designed a computer operating system that puts Apple and Windows to shame. Like many of those successful in business, you've decided to build yourself a custom home.

You've found a nice chunk of land and intend to build your marvelous new home on the side of a hill overlooking a bay in some well-to-do area. You call a builder and tell him your budget for your new mansion is roughly $2 million. You've drawn a couple of pictures on looseleaf of what you would like your house to look like and you hand them over to the builder. He smiles and says, "Looks great. But I can't use these."

As a demanding and successful person, you look at the builder a little puzzled and ask him what he means. He answers, "You need to contact an architect, an engineer, a land surveyor, and a lawyer."

You have a vague understanding of what an architect does for a living: they design buildings. But an engineer and a land surveyor? An engineer, like a guy who drives a train? A land surveyor? You vaguely remember that you read somewhere that Founding Fathers such as George Washington and Thomas Jefferson were "land surveyors," but you're not quite sure what a land surveyor does.

Above all, what do you need a lawyer for? Last you checked, lawyers don't swing hammers and build homes.

Different Professions for Building a House

Engineering, or more specifically civil engineering, concerns itself with structures such as buildings, houses, bridges, roads, sewage systems, stadiums, race tracks, and concerns itself with areas of study including traffic flow. The running track at your school was plotted by an engineer and leveled by a land surveyor. Military engineers do similar work for the armed forces. Engineering degrees are usually four-year degrees that specialized in an area of interest such as drainage or structural (or both). Engineers then must be licensed by the state in which they work in order to earn a living.

A land surveyor is somebody who measures land, takes topographic surveys that include locating trees and other "natural land monuments," as well as performing title surveys that mark land boundaries and identify the landowner. Land surveyors also take elevations on land so that houses and buildings can be laid out with the floors being level. In other words, engineers and land surveyors are the primary reason why your classroom floor is level and your desk stands flat and is not sliding down the hallway. To become a land surveyor, you need to complete a four year college degree and also become licensed by the state in which you work.

Lawyers come into play because while the architect may design your house, the engineer will make sure it is properly built according to specifications ("specs," as they say on construction sites), and the land surveyor will make sure your eggs don't roll off your kitchen table, a lawyer is needed to appear before the local "Zoning Board" to make sure it complies with your town's building specifications and codes.

For example, houses built in earthquake or tornado zones have different building specifications than houses built along the east coast. Depending on your local town or city government, there are certain rules and regulations local municipalities pass that they feel are for public safety. New constructions usually need to be presented to the local government for approval and some new constructions may require a "variance," where the builder needs to appeal to the local government for a dispensation.

Along with local building codes, there are also state and Federal laws that must be considered. For example, the Federal Emergency Management Agency (FEMA) requires that buildings and homes meet certain standards for first floor elevations in area where coastal flooding poses a threat. Home and building owners who comply with FEMA standards save money on insurance rates.

So now your $2 million dollar customized home may cost more like $2.25 million once you've paid the architect, engineer, land surveyor, lawyer and whatever fees your local municipality charges for new construction permits and the like.

The Task: Organizing SmartArt

SmartArt Graphic Organizer

Create a new Excel file and name it appropriately and in the correct area on your computer/network drive. Label the worksheet "House Graphic Organizer." We're going to create a simple hierarchical graphic organizer labeling the various professionals we need to hire for building the new house.

SmartArt Hierarchal Graphic Organizer

Excel provides "SmartArt" (see **Figure 18.2**) a way of creating graphic charts that can be used for a number of functions, such as hierarchical structures, cycles, lists, workflow processes, and a host of other means of depicting information through the use of graphics. There is even a way of importing your own photos or graphics and including them in the SmartArt templates.

These graphics can also be copied-and-pasted into other programs, including Microsoft Word and PowerPoint. In fact, PowerPoint has the same "SmartArt" tool. And yes, these SmartArt graphics can be copied-

and-pasted into non-Microsoft programs such as Adobe Photoshop and Illustrator.

Our "Graphic Organizer" is going to be a simple visual list of what professionals we're going to need to build our millionaire's mansion. You might even question why we're doing this at all, but the answer is simple: just to gain experience working with and editing SmartArt. We're going to start off with a hierarchal chart .

In the Windows version of Excel, the SmartArt button is in the Insert tab. On the Mac, SmartArt has its own tab. Select the Hierarchy option and then select "Table Hierarchy." A blank template of a hierarchal chart will appear with placeholder text over each box. A text entry box will appear to the left of the graphic (see **Figure 18.3**, next page).

Editing SmartArt

You can input labels directly into the text boxes that appear over the graphic or use the text entry box on the left side called "Text Pane." We're going to use the Text Pane because this is the most efficient approach.

By using the Enter/Return key in the Text Pane, you can add more boxes to your chart. By hitting the delete key, you can remove a box. By using the tab key, you can move the boxes so they appear below the level you are currently at. By clicking on the "x" in the upper-left corner of the Text Pane (see again **Figure 18.3**, next page), the box will close. To open it, click on the small icon in the upper-left and it will re-appear.

In our case, we want to place the architect at the top of the hierarchy, the engineer below the architect, and the land surveyor and builder below the engineer. Then we want to place the lawyer, on equal footing with the engineer, below the architect on the right side and then,

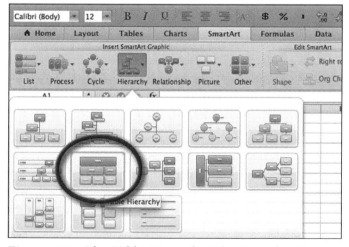

Figure 18.2: The Table Hierarchy Chart on the Mac. In Windows, the SmartArt button is located in the Insert tab.

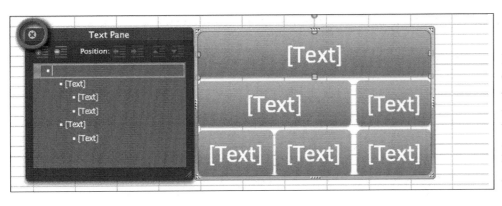

Figure 18.3: The Table Hierarchy Chart with the Text Pane. To close the Text Pane, click on the "x" on the upper-left corner. Information can be input either directly where the placeholder text is [Text] or in the Text Pane. It is recommended that you use the Text Pane.

In the top box field area of the Text Pane, enter "Architect." For now, avoid using the Enter/Return key. Hitting the Enter/Return key will only add more graphic boxes to your hierarchal chart, which we don't want to do for now. Instead, use your mouse/cursor to go to the next field area in the text entry box and type in, "Engineer."

Use your mouse/cursor to go to the next field area and enter "Land Surveyor." And, using your mouse, click to the next field and enter, "Builder/Contractor" (see **Figure 18.5**).

Use your mouse/cursor and go down to the next level in the Text Pane and input "Lawyer" and then "Town Zoning Board." To get out of the Text Pane, click on any random cell outside the hierarchal template.

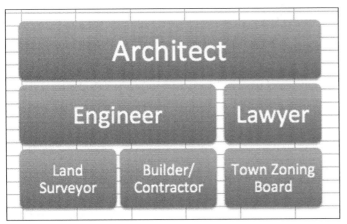

Figure 18.4: Your Table Hierarchal Chart should look something like this when you are finished.

below the lawyer, we'll input "Town Zoning Board" to demonstrate the lawyer will be dealing with the Town Zoning Board (see **Figure 18.4** for an idea of what our hierarchal chart will look like).

Adding More Professionals

Looks good so far, but you realized you forgot to add the pool building company and the landscape architect. Both need to consult with the Architect and Engineer,

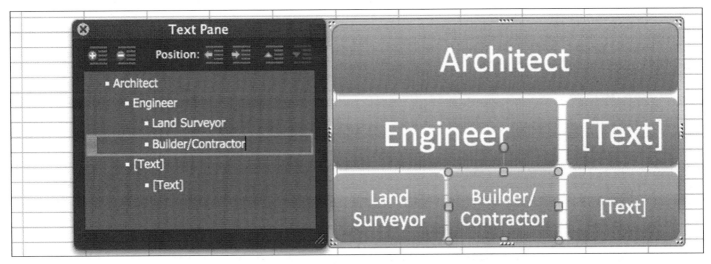

Figure 18.5: Using the Text Pane for inputting information in your graphic organizer. By hitting the Enter/Return key, you can add another box. By using the tab key, you can add another sub-category in the hierarchy. By deleting, you can remove a box and/or category.

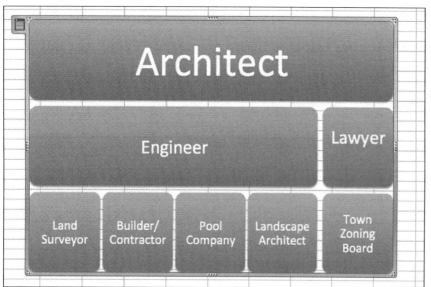

Figure 18.6: By striking the Enter/Return key in the Text Pane beneath the "Builder/Contractor" entry, you can add the "Pool Company." Strike the Enter/Return key once again and you can add another sub-category, "Landscape Architect." The graphic organizer can be enlarged (or reduced) the same way any graphic is sized in Microsoft programs: hover your mouse to the upper-left or lower-right corner, wait for the cursor to convert into the diagonal double-headed arrow, .and then click-and-drag.

so you want to add these two professionals on the Engineer side. Select (click) back on the hierarchal graphic and the Text Pane will re-appear. Select the text "Builder/Contractor" and hit the enter/return key. A new box will appear to the right of "Builder/Contractor." Enter "Pool Company." Now strike the enter/return key once again, another box will appear and input "Landscape Architect."

Close the Text Pane and enlarge the graphic by hovering your mouse cursor over the right corner, waiting for it to turn into a diagonal double-headed arrow, and clicking-and-dragging downwards to expand the graphic (**Figure 18.6** will give you an idea of what the chart should now look like enlarged and after you've added "Pool Company" and "Landscape Architect" to the Text Pane).

If you change your mind and decide not to have a pool, go into the Text Pane and delete "Pool Company." The boxes will readjust themselves.

Changing Chart Styles

So far so good? But as you look at your hierarchal chart, you want it to demonstrate the hierarchal relationships more definitively. So let's change the chart style. First, click on the chart. Next, go back into the Hierarchy button (Mac) or select the SmartArt button in Windows. Now select "Name and Title Organization Chart" (it's usually the second selection; see **Figure 18.7**).

This hierarchal chart will draw lines showing the relationships to each box category. It will also give you another text box so you may enter people's names or other

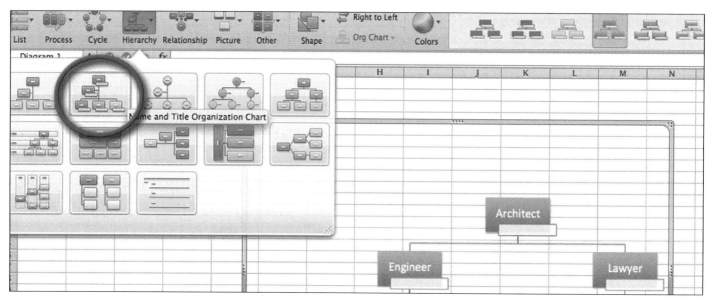

Figure 18.7: Excel allows you to change chart styles by simply clicking on an existing chart and then selecting a different chart style in the SmartArt button or tab.

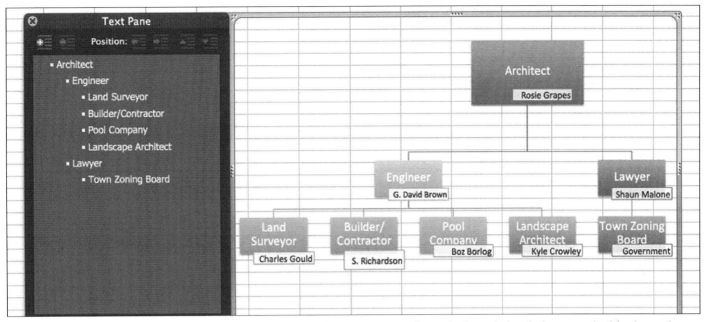

Figure 18.8: In the "Name and Title Organization Chart," input names of people directly by clicking on the blank text boxes and inputing a name.

identifying labels. To input the names, you have to click directly into the new text boxes. Make up some names and input them into each professional (see **Figure 18.8**).

Changing Colors, Sizes, and Adding Effects

The colors, sizes, and effects of the parts of your hierarchal chart can be individually altered. Click on the box that reads "Architect." Now hover the cursor to the upper-left corner, wait for it to change to the double-headed diagonal arrow and click-and-drag upwards to enlarge.

You can move the individual boxes "manually" by clicking on a box and dragging it to where you wish. You can also move the text boxes that contain the fake names you gave your architect, engineer, land surveyor, etc.

Right-click (Control + click, Mac). A popup menu will appear. Select "Format Shape" and experiment. You can change the boxes' colors and even put a pattern in the background. You can add 3-D effects and even change the 3-D angel of the boxes. You can apply drop shadows and add filters. (see **Figure 18.9**).

You can also change color schemes by selecting the entire hierarchal graphic and then selecting one of the pre-set color schemes Excel offers in the Colors button (see **Figure 18.10**).

Fool around. Play. Experiment. See what drop shadows and other functions do for your graphic organizer.

Keep in mind that further projects using SmartArt and graphic organizers must be well-planned before attempting this in Excel. A piece of scrap paper and pencil may come in handy for planning your graphics beforehand.

And congratulations on your foray into the exciting world of "Smart Art."

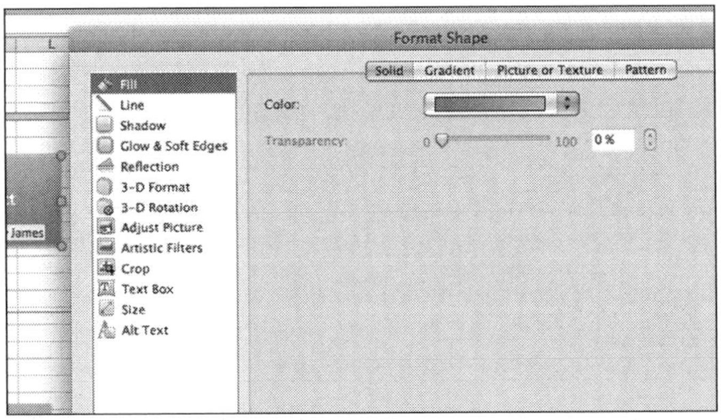

Figure 18.9: The "Format Shape" palette.

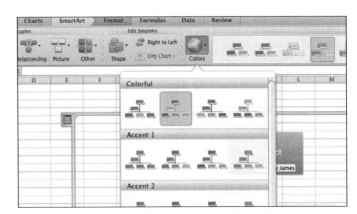

Figure 18.10: Preset color schemes on the Mac.

19 Section III: HTML
Urban Legends:
A Simple Web Page

Figure 19.1: For this project, we're going to do a simple Web page that layout wise, will look like this. It's a simple Web page comprising text, an image, and links. Behind the screenshot of the Web page is the HTML coding.

I N THE MID-1970S, there was a television commercial for Life Cereal featuring three brothers wary of eating the new cereal their mom bought home. The two older brothers kept pushing the bowl to one another saying, "I'm not gonna try it. You try it." After a few rounds of this, one of the brothers had the idea to pass the bowl to the youngest brother, Mikey, who shoveled his spoon right into the cereal and began devouring it. One of the older brothers observed, "Hey Mikey! He likes it!"

And thus, a new catch-phrase was entered into the American vernacular: any boy or man named Mike during the 1970s through the 1980s more than likely heard somebody say, "Hey Mikey! He likes it!"

A few years after the Mikey craze, a story began to circulate about little Mikey: he ate a package of Pop Rocks and washed it down with soda and unfortunately exploded. Quite a few people believed this story but it was totally false: to date, little Mikey is still alive and

works in the advertising industry. And just in case, no, you will not explode if you eat a package of Pop Rocks and wash it down with soda, although it may make you profusely sneeze and burp.

Also around the same time in the mid-1970s, a new type of gum was invented called Bubble Yum. It was soft and easy to chew. Prior to this, gum was hard and the chewer had to "work it" in order to get it going. Bubble Yum was an American success story: it was a new product that people, mainly kids, loved. It became wildly popular as did bubble blowing contests in Major League Baseball dugouts across America.

Towards the mid-to-late 1970s, a story began circulating that the people who make Bubble Yum use spider eggs to make the gum soft. One version of the spider egg story claimed that the spider eggs were exotic and from South America. These spider eggs would attach themselves to the inside of the cheek and then hatch when the chewer was asleep at night. The chewer would wake up to discover hundreds of spiders crawling out of his or her mouth.

The spider egg story spread like wildfire and negatively impacted sales of Bubble Yum. The manufacturers had to take out full page ads in newspapers to dispel the spider egg rumor.

Both the Mikey from the Life Cereal commercial and the Bubble Yum story are examples of Urban Legends. In the case of little Mikey, he really didn't appear in many TV commercials after the Life Cereal advertisement and since he fell out of the public eye, it was conceivable that something horrible happened to him. In the case of Bubble Yum, what was the "magic" behind the great tasting and soft bubble gum? It had to be "something." The stories were also believable considering the target audience: middle school aged kids.

An urban legend is generally a shocking or weird story that some people believe is true. Sometimes, the story is so strange it is believable, or the story is so shockingly horrific it "has to be true." The types of stories told in urban legends range from humorous to weird to frighteningly freakish. There are many urban legends surrounding products, celebrities, and politicians.

The Task

You are to create a Web page that features an Urban Legend of your own creation. The Web page should have the following:

1. A headline using the H1 Header.
2. A byline using the H3 Header.
3. Colored text (blue, green, etc.). The Headline should be in a colored font.
4. The background color changed (the default background color is white). Stay away from using black for a background color.
5. One image that illustrates your urban legend.
6. An image caption using the H4 header.
7. At least three paragraphs telling the story in news writing style (inverted pyramid, described below).
8. Bolded text—pick a word or two that you wish to appear bolded.
9. Italicized text—pick a word or two that you wish to italicize.
10. Two links to other Web sites.

First, create a folder and name it "Number_Last-Name_UrbanLegend." Second, create a Microsoft Word file and save it into that folder with the same naming convention: "Number_LastName_UrbanLegend."

Second, open up your newly created folder and create another folder inside it. Name it "images". Your folders should resemble the folders in **Figures 19.2** (Windows) and **19.3** (Mac).

Next, write your Urban Legend. It should be three paragraphs long (although you may make it longer if you wish) and somewhat convincing. After you've written your story, find or create an image that best depicts your story. Make sure you save this image in the images folder.

Your Word document should begin with a headline followed by your byline (by Sally Jones, for example) on the next line. Then your three paragraphs should be written in journalistic, news-style (inverted pyramid first paragraph: Who, what, where, when, and why lead the story). There is no need to bold or stylize any fonts while you are working in Microsoft Word. This will be done with HTML codes.

If you need story ideas, go to a search engine (Google, Yahoo!, BING, etc.) and type in "Urban Legend." Although Snopes.com is considered a reliable Web site when it comes to debunking most urban legends, some people complain that Snopes has a leftwing bias and distorts issues whenever the authors cover politics.

Once you are finished writing your urban legend, you can begin to build and edit your Web page using HTML.

HTML

HTML is the acronym for HyperText Markup Language. "Hypertext" simply means that a computer end user—that is you—can create a link to another Web

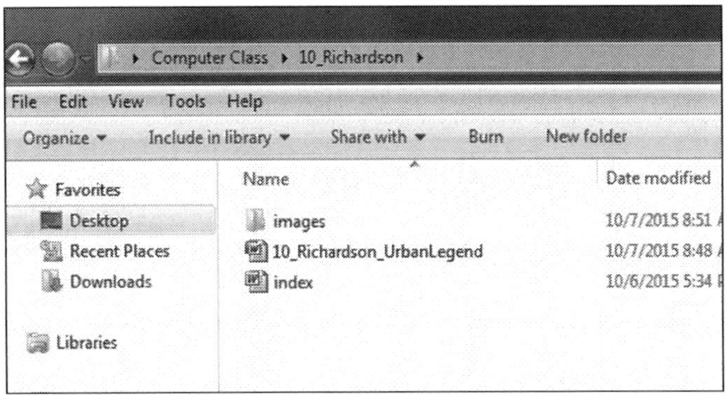

Figure 19.2: Folder organization for HTML project in Windows.

Figure 19.3: Folder organization for HTML project on the Mac.

page within an HTML document. HyperText Markup Language's main quality is its universality, meaning that HTML documents are saved in ASCII (pronounced "askie") text so that any computer can read a Web page.

How a Web page appears not only depends on the skills of the Web designer, but it also depends on the computers and Web browsers being used.

Some Web sites may appear differently on an Apple Computer than on a Windows PC, especially if those computers are older models. Also, Web pages may appear differently because of certain settings on the Web surfer's computer, like the font size or zoom settings.

Like all computer languages and programs, every little detail is important in HTML. An accidentally deleted quote mark or an extra space between letters can make your code unworkable. Be careful not to accidentally highlight a quote mark and delete it or that you do not inadvertly add extra spaces.

HTML utilizes a series of "tags" that are commands to Web browsers, explaining what the Web page should look like. These tags begin with an "angle bracket" or "less than" symbol, <. The tags end with a closing angle bracket or the "greater than" symbol, >. Each one of these tags tells the Web browser how things should appear on a Web page.

Each command has an opening tag and a closing tag. For example, the tag to make a word boldface is . To close the tag so that the rest of the text does not appear bolded, you would place a after the text you wished to make bold. For example: dog

Web Browsers

A Web browser is a program that reads HTML and other files that are coded for the World Wide Web. Browsers basically translate HTML-coded files so they can appear clearly to the Web viewer (client). Mac computers come with a browser named Safari; Windows PCs come with InternetExplorer. Firefox is another popular Web browser that is available for both Windows and Macs. All of these Web browsers are "free" (the cost is factored into the price of the operating system and/or computer or through advertising and donations for Firefox).

In Windows, if you click on the View menu on your browser and scroll to where it reads "View Source," a simple text file will appear displaying the HTML code used to build that Web page. Yes, the text can be copied-and-pasted and edited, but this will not make changes to the Web page that exists on the Internet. In order to change a Web page that is live on the Internet, you need a password to get to the server where the Web page resides. Doing this illegally is called "hacking."

For the Mac, to view the source code for a Web page, make sure the Develop menu appears in the menu bar. If the Develop menu is not present, go into the Safari menu, select Preferences, go to the Advanced tab and select "Show Develop menu in menu bar" located at the bottom of the dialog box. Once the Develop menu appears in the menu bar, select "Show Page Source."

TextEdit and WordPad: Simple Text Editors Used for Writing Code

On the Mac, HTML can be coded and edited in a program called TextEdit, which comes "free" with every Apple. If TextEdit is not on the Dock, go into the Applications folder and double-click the TextEdit icon to launch the program. To keep TextEdit in the dock, click-and-hold your mouse over the icon on the dock, wait for a dialog box to appear and select "Options." In the "Options" area, make sure to check off "Keep in Dock."

In Windows, HTML can be coded and edited in a program called WordPad, which comes "free" with every Windows operating system. To get to WordPad on the PC, go into the Start menu, select "All Programs," scroll to "Accessories," and then select WordPad. Most HTML experts prefer to use "NotePad," but using this program can be cumbersome and we're going to begin by using WordPad.

> *Note:* For Mac users, "curly quotes" can ruin a line of code, as these quote marks are special characters and not "basic" characters. This includes quote marks and apostrophes. Before getting started, launch TextEdit, go into the TextEdit menu, select "Preferences" and make sure the "Smart Quotes" is not selected (see **Figure 19.4**, next page).

> *Note:* Although Microsoft Word can edit and create HTML files, it is not the most proficient program for HTML editing. A simple text editor is preferred. For our purposes here, we are going to avoid using MS Word.

Getting Started

Launch WordPad (Windows) or TextEdit (Mac), select "Save," name the file "index" and be sure to navigate to your newly created folder and save it inside that directory. The "index" file should be right next to the "images" folder created earlier (see again, **Figures 19.2** and **19.3**). In your WordPad or TextEdit document, enter the following text as shown on the following page:

```
<!DOCTYPE html>
<html>
<head>
    <title>Page Title</title>
</head>
    <body>
        <body bgcolor="white">
        <h1 style="color:black"> This is a Heading: use for your story's headline</h1>
        <h3>by Your Name</h3>
        <img src="images/picture.jpg"alt="picture" style="width:373px;height:360px;">
        <h4>This is your photo caption</h4>
                <p>First paragraph.</p>
                <p>Second paragraph.</p>
                <p>Third paragraph.</p>
        <a href="http://www.WebsiteName.com">Name of Link</a>
        <a href="http://www.WebsiteName.com">Name of Link</a>
    </body>
</html>
```

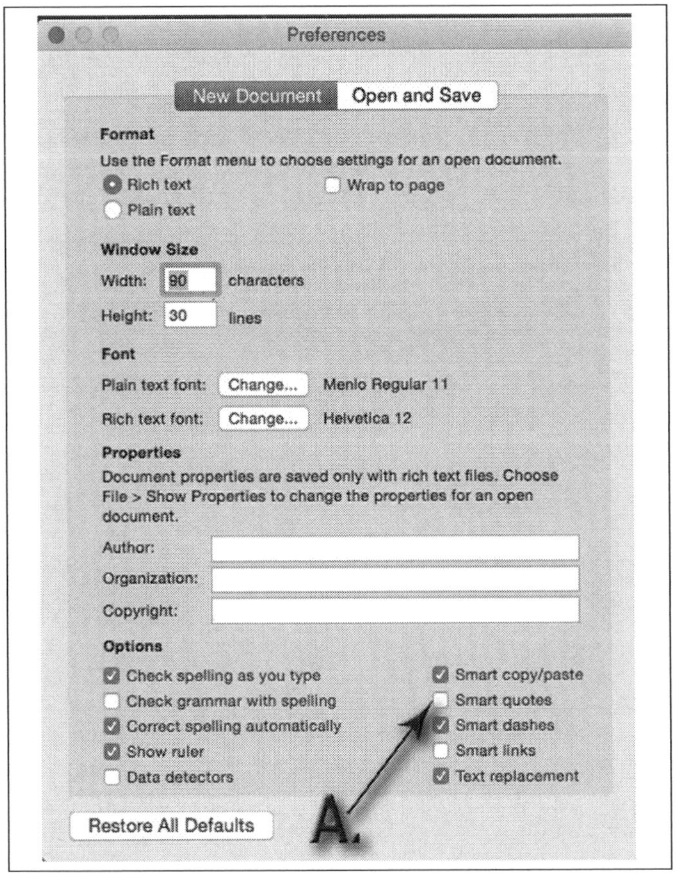

Figure 19.4: Mac users, make sure the "Smart Quotes" option is NOT checked off in the TextEdit Preferences (A.).

Hexadecimal Equivalent Colors

HTML uses a set of numbers called Hexadecimal Equivalents to achieve color in a web page. These colors are variations of the RGB mode—red, green, and blue. An extensive list of Hexadecimal Equivalents can be found on Wikipedia. In order for them to work, the pound sign (#) needs to be placed in front of the color's number. For example, an off-red color would read as #FF4D4D in between the quote marks where the word "white" currently appears.

Checking Image Sizes

To check the image size in Windows, go into the images folder, select the image and then right-click on the image. A popup menu will appear. Select "Properties" listed at the bottom. A dialog box will appear next. Make sure you select the Details tab. The dimensions will appear in the Image area in the dialog box.

To check the image size on a Mac, click on the image file to select it and then hit "Command + I." The image dimensions should appear in the upper portion of the information box.

Image Formats for the Internet

There are at least three widely used image formats for the Internet images: .jpg, .gif, and .png. These image identifying tags must be used in your code.

A Breakdown of the HTML Tags Used for this Project

Take note of the difference between curly or smart quotes, that look like this: " " and this: ' ' and "ASCII" quotes, which are straight, like this: " " and ' '. Also note that indenting is done only to differentiate and keep track of the HTML lines. See **Figure 19.5** on this page and the following page for reference.

A. <!DOCTYPE html> This tag describes to the Web browser what type of document it is.

B. <head> and </head> These tags identify the "Head" container in HTML. This is where scripts (like JavaScript) and other instructions are placed for the Web page (like the page's title, etc.). Also contained within the Head area is metadata, such as keywords and information for search engines like Google.

C. <title> and </title> Between these two tags input the text that will appear in the Web browser. In the example provided here, "Mummy Attacks Man" will appear in the browser's title bar.

D. <body> This tag declares where all the elements (text, photos, links, etc.) will appear in the Web browser. It will close out towards the bottom (see Letter O.).

E. <body bgcolor="white"> This tag determines the body's background color. In the example provided here, the background will be white. There are 16 pre-determined Web colors that can be input: Silver, Gray, Maroon, Green, Navy, Purple, Olive, Teal, White, Black, Red, Lime, Blue, Magenta, Yellow, and Cyan. These are the colors we will be using for the Urban Legends project.

F. <h1> </h1> This is an H1 head. There are six headers in HTML: H1, H2, H3, H4, H5, and H6. H1 is the largest while H6 is the smallest.

G. <h1 style="color:black"> This is an example of a "nested command:" extra instructions within a set of tags. The color appears in the quote marks followed by a closing bracket, >. The headline's text appears and then the command is ended with the H1 closing tag, </h1>.

H. <h3> and </h3> An H3 tag for your byline.

i. <img src="images/mummy.jpg" alt="mummy" style="width:373px;height:360px;"> This line of code declares where the image is, what the image name is, and the image size. The "images/"

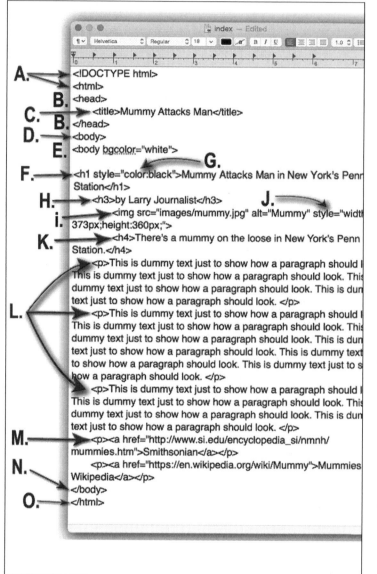

Figure 19.5: A breakdown of the HTML code. When you're ready to edit the HTML, be precise and place your text between the appropriate tags.

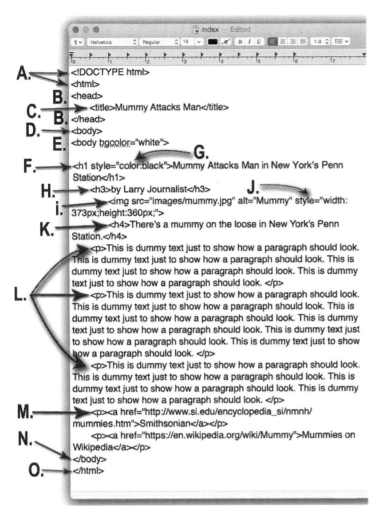

Figure 19.5: (*continued*). A breakdown of the HTML code.

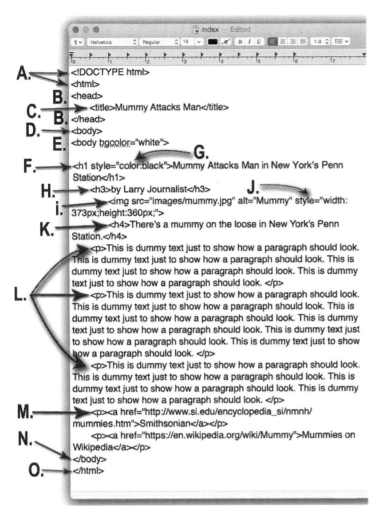

Figure 19.6: Windows users, to get the size of an image, right-click on the file while in your job folder. Select "Properties," click on the "Details" tab, and go to the Image area of the dialog box.

part identifies where the image is saved: in this case, it is saved inside the "images" folder you created at the beginning of this project. Immediately following the forward slash (/) is the name of the image with its image identifying tag, .jpg. In this case the name of the file is "mummy.jpg" (see **Letter J.**). The "alt" part of the code (alt="mummy") will display the image name should the image not be able to load.

J. The style="width:373px;height:360px;"> is the part of the code gives the pixel dimensions of the image. Images can be resized as long as they are resized proportionately. If we were to reduce the size of this image, we would subtract 100 pixels from both the width and height (273 x 260). If resizing is not done in equal proportion, then the image will appear warped. To check the size of a figure in Windows, see **Figure 19.6**. To check the size of a figure on the Mac, See **Figure 19.7**.

K. <h4> H4 header.

L. <p> Begins a paragraph, </p> ends a paragraph. Copy and paste your first paragraph between these, the second paragraph between the second set of paragraph commands and the third paragraph between the third set. If you wrote an extra paragraph or two, you can add extra paragraphs as well.

M. <p> Once again, begins a paragraph. The <a href="http://www.si.edu/encyclopedia_si/nmnh/mummies.htm">Smithsonian</a> is a "hot link" command. The first part, <a href="http://www.si.edu/encyclopedia_si/nmnh/mummies.htm"> gives the full Web address URL (Uniform Resource Locator). It will not appear on the page. The second part of the tag after the closing bracket >, Smithsonian</a>, is what appears on the page. Some people call this a "callout."

N. </body> This tag closes the body area.

O. </html> This tag tells the browser that there is no more to the document. It's over.

Creating an HTML File in Windows

Once you are finished editing your "index" file, make sure to save it. If you don't save it first, you'll lose the edits and changes you made. So again, save the file. After saving the file, go into the File menu and select "Save As."

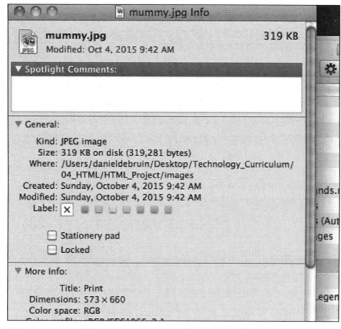

Figure 19.7: Mac users, to get the size of an image, select the file while in your job folder and then hit "Command + I." The pixel dimensions will appear in the "More Info" area of the dialog box.

In the lower portion of the "Save As" dialog box, you see "Save as type:". Click on the bar and select "Text Document" (see **Figure 19.8**). Make sure you keep the name "index" and add a .html to the file so it looks like, index. html. Be sure to close the file after you finished.

Navigate to your folder. Double-click on the index. html file. Microsoft Internet Explorer should launch. You should be able to see your Web page in the browser.

If there are any mistakes, go back and check over your code.

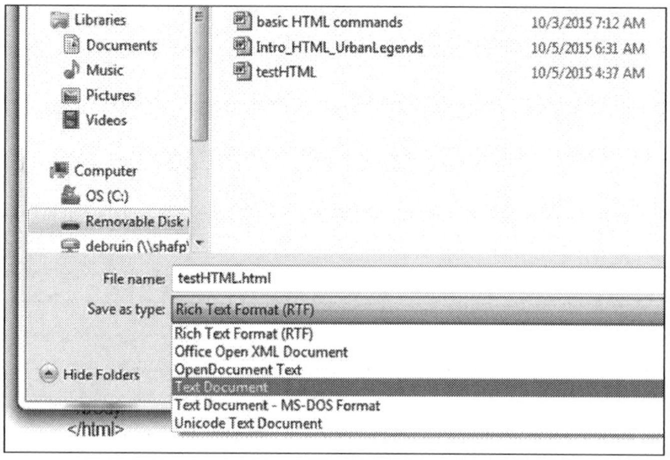

Figure 19.8: Windows users, after saving your work, go into File>>Save As. The "Save As" dialog box will appear. Click on the "Save as type:" area in the lower portion of the dialog box and select "Text Document."

Creating an HTML File on the Mac

In previous editions of Apple's TextEdit, converting text to HTML used to be a lot simpler. For some strange reason, Apple made things a lot more complicated.

First, when you are finished editing and working with the HTML tags, save your work.

Next, go into the File menu and select "Duplicate". A new, duplicate file will "bounce" in front of the original, prompting you to rename it (see **Figure 19.9**). Don't rename it just yet. Click on the original file (index) and close it to avoid confusion.

Now go into the Format menu and select "Make Plain Text." Go back into the File menu and select "Rename…" A dialog box will appear with a "Save As:" prompt. Look at the bottom of the dialog box and make sure to deselect the checkbox in front of "If no extension is provided, use ".txt" (see **Figure 19.10**).

Return to the "Save As:" area. It should say "index copy." Delete the word "copy", go right to the end of the word "index," and add .html after it. It should look like this: index.html

Your index.html file's icon should change (to that of a Safari icon). Navigate to your project folder, double-click on the index.html file and view it in Safari. If there are any errors, go back and edit or fix those errors. Remember to save your changes first and then go convert the text file by going to "Save As."

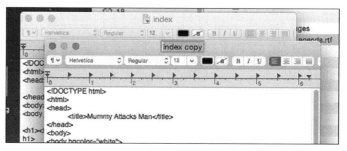

Figure 19.9: Mac users, after selecting "Duplicate" from the File menu, a copy of your original file (index) will "bounce" in front of the original. Don't rename it just yet. First close the original file and then go into the duplicate, select the Format menu, and chose "Make Plain Text."

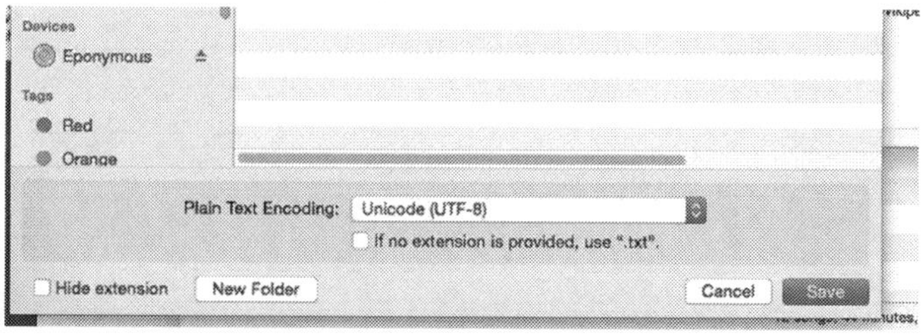

Figure 19.10: Mac users, make sure to uncheck the box next to "If no extension is provided, use ".txt." Then name the file, "index.html."

Now that you've successfully completed your first round, let's make some edits and some easy changes.

Bolding and Italicizing Text

Pick out one random word and bold it. To bold the word, use the <b> and </b> tags. To italicize a word, pick out a random word and use the <i> and </i> tags.

Changing Font Colors

To change the font color of the headline to green, go to the h1 tag <h1>. Input <h1 style="color:green">. If you prefer red or any of the other standard 16 colors, make sure you follow the example just provided.

Black Background

If you want a black background, you're going to have to change all the text color to white so it can be read. Before doing that, make sure you change the <body bgcolor> tag to <body bgcolor="black">. Then go into each of the header tags and follow the example above: <h1 style="color:white">. To change the text in the body paragraphs, input: <p style="color:white">.

Not "Live"

The HTML file you created is not "live." You are viewing the file "locally" from your hard drive. In order for the Web page to be live, you need access to a Web server and then the files need to be uploaded. We'll get into that later.

Notes

_____

_____

_____

_____

_____

_____

_____

_____

_____

_____

_____

_____

_____

Index

A

Apple Computers 14–16
Application 31
Archiving a Web Page 31, 42

B

Binary language 18
Binary Language 31
block-style business letter 34
Business Letter 32

C

Catholic Church 19
Citing a Source 25
   Citing a Web Page 26
   direct quote 26
   Framing a Quote 27
   paraphrased quote 26
Command + F (Mac); Control + F (Windows)
   Searching a Web Page 42
CPU
   Central Processing Unit 17–18

D

Directory 12–13

E

E. Remington and Sons 14
Excel
   adjust the size of a row 35
   Basic Functions 35
   see Microsoft Excel 67
Expository Paper 47
   Body Paragraphs 48
   Concluding Paragraph 48
   Introduction Paragraph 47
   Punctuation 49
   Topic Sentence 47
   Transitional Words and Phrases 48

F

File Management 11–13
Fonts palette 59

G

General Search in a Program
   Control F, Windows; Command F, Mac 31
Glidden, Carlos 14–16

H

HTML 94
   acronym 95
   Bolding and Italicizing Text 101
   Changing Font Colors 101
   curly quotes 96
   Folder organization 95
   Hexadecimal Equivalent Colors 97
   Image Formats 97
   Image Sizes 97
   tags 96
   TextEdit (Mac) 96
   Web browser function 96
   WordPad (Windows) 96

I

Invisible Characters 21

K

Keyboarding 14–16
King Henry VIII 19

L

Local Area Network
   LAN 11

M

Mail Merge 32
   Complete Merge 37

Finish & Merge, Windows 38
Insert Placeholders 36
Mail Merge Manager 36
Microsoft Corporation 16
Microsoft Excel
   Applying borders 72
   Applying Formulas to Columns 69
   Autosum Tool 75, 84
   Charts
      Adding a Chart Title 84
      Editing a Text Legend on a Chart 87
      Format Chart Legend 87
      Quick Layouts 84
   Clearing Contents 67
   Fitting Text into Cells
      Wrap Text 76
   Format a Column
      apply formatting functions 73
   Format Cells 67
   Format Rows
      apply formatting functions 73
   Formatting numbers 70
   Formula Bar 74
   Home Ribbon 72
   Inserting Columns and Rows
      Deleting Columns and Rows 84
   Landscape a document 85
   Lock Columns or Rows
      Scrolling
         Freeze Panes 75
   Merge cells 76
   Ribbon preferences palette 73
   running head 85
   Setting Formulas 69
   SmartArt
      Adding entries 91
      Changing Chart Styles 92
      Changing Colors, Sizes, and Adding Effects 93
      Editing SmartArt 90
      Graphic Organizer 90
         Hierarchal Graphic Organizer 90

SmartArt (*continued*)
  Text Pane 91
SmartArt Charts 89
Sort tool 74
  Text Alignment 75
Microsoft Word 11–13
  Aligning Text, Line Spacing, and Indents 22
  Creating a Works Cited Page 25
  Font dialogue box 21
  Insert Page Break 28
  Move Image Behind or In Front of Text
    Wrap Text 59
  Page Number 24
  Page Numbers dialogue box 23
  Paragraph Formatting 22
  Running Head 23
  Setting "Tab stops" 58
  Working in Columns 56
    leader line 56
    Soft Return 58
  Working with Tables 60
    Academic Table
      Table Footnote 65
    Insert an Image in a Table 61
    Table Control
      Move Tables 61

Wrapping Text
  Move Image in front or behind text 62
MLA
  Modern Language Association 19
MLA Formatting 19, 43
  Badge 19
  Works Cited Entries 54
More, Thomas 19
Motherboard 31

N

Network Drive 11

O

OS
  Operating System 18

P

Paragraph Dialog Box 22
Paragraph Formatting palette 22
  Hanging Indent 29
Paragraph Formatting Palette
  Setting up a Hanging Indent 41
Plagiarism 25

Q

QWERTY 14–16

R

RAM (Random Access Memory) 31

S

Select All 31
Setting up Stylesheets 51
  New Styles 52
  Style palette 51
Sholes, Christopher Latham 14
Smart Quotes 97
Storage Memory 31

U

USB (Universal Serial Bus) 31
Utopia
  More, Thomas 20

W

WordArt 59